What crisis communication leaders are saying about the One Page Crisis Communication Playbook

"Truly the best work I've read on the discipline of crisis communications, because it is about communicating with stakeholders rather than just focusing on 'media management'. It sets a new standard."

Neil Chapman
CEO, Alpha Voice Communications
Former BP Communications Executive

"I just read the One Page Crisis Communications Playbook, and all I can say is "WOW!". As an experienced incident commander with the unique experience as an early adopter of social media tools for crisis response, I was more than impressed with Gerald's insight and practical advice for those entrusted with managing crisis. His public relations experience, political savvy, understanding of the new world of communications and practical incident command work is reflected in this succinct, easy to understand playbook. He 'gets it,' has 'lived it,' and now is helping others succeed in managing crisis. Well done."

Chief Bill Boyd
Fire Chief, Incident Commander, Social Media Expert

"In the high stakes arena of crisis communication, there are invariably winners and losers. Gerald Baron's new "Playbook" provides an unparalleled and indispensable guide to preserving an organization's reputation. Baron's battle-tested approach, correctly implemented, will enable any communications executive to answer 'yes' when the CEO asks if the company is prepared for a worst case public relations nightmare."

George F. Smalley
CEO, Bridge Builder Communications
Former Shell, Saudi Aramco, and Harris County (Houston) Metro communication executive

OnePage Crisis Communication Playbook

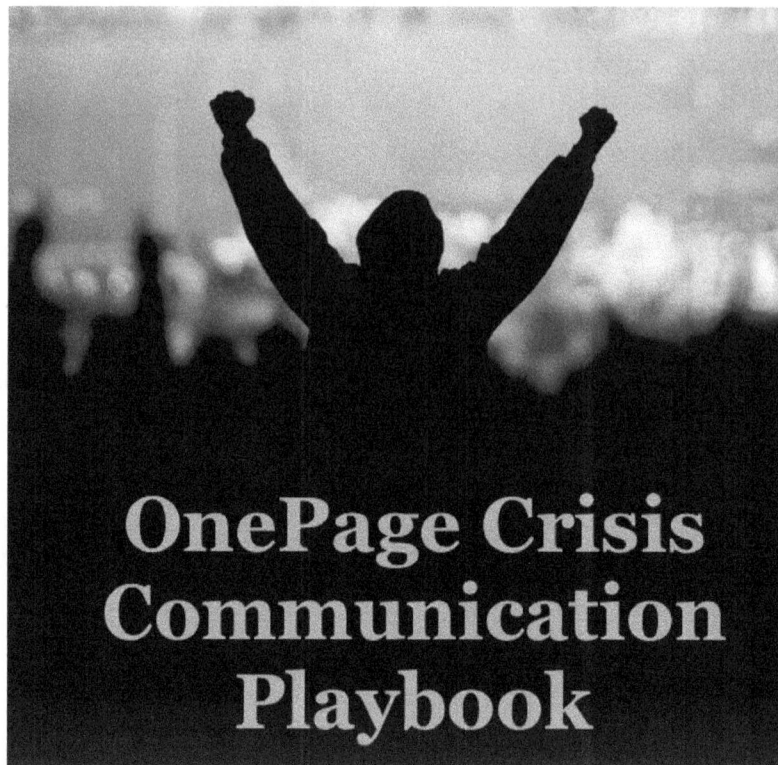

The OnePage Crisis Communication Playbook Manual

© 2012 by Gerald Baron

PDF version
1.   Version: 2.0CS

Published by Edens Veil Media
in association with Agincourt Strategies LLC
www.agincourt.us

1319 Cornwall Ave.
Suite 201
Bellingham, WA 98225
training@agincourt.us

Event

Step 1
Notifications

Front line call
9-1-1 if needed
Response team activated
Communication Lead activated
Initial assessment

Step 2
Initial Message

Key facts: What, where, injuries, response, empathy, next communication.

Channels?

Holding statement, publish, publish and send?

Step 3
Assessment

How bad is it?
How bad could it get?

Green--Monitor
Yellow--Low Response
Red--High Response

Strategy: Reactive, Low Proactive, High Proactive

Step 4
Team Activation

Green-Standby notice

Yellow-Small team (media or stakeholder focused)

Red--Large team (media or stakeholder focused)

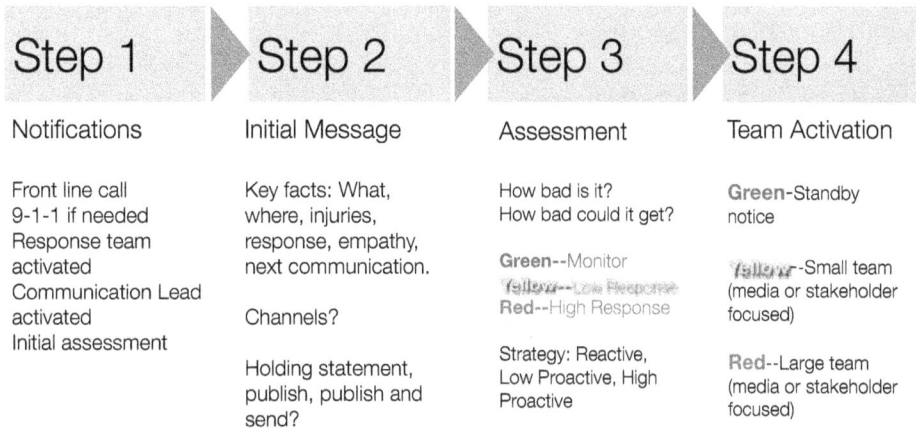

Step 5 Workflow

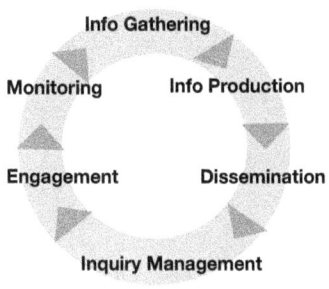

Info Gathering

Monitoring   Info Production

Engagement   Dissemination

Inquiry Management

Comm Lead
— Spokesperson(s)
— Support
— Information Gathering/ Monitoring
— Information Production
— Dissemination
— Inquiry Management
— Stakeholder Engagement

Step 6

Transitions and Deactivation

1. Prepare critical staffing for long term events.
2. Allow sufficient transition periods.
3. Declining media coverage does not mean declining communication.
4. Events with external impact require long term engagement and continued communications.

Guidelines

General Guidelines

1. Safety first.
2. Our goal is building trust.
3. Timely, accurate information required.
4. Actions speak louder than words.
5. The media and public have a right to know.
6. Transparency and honesty are essential.
7. Respond quickly to rumors.
8. We will respond to questions & comments.
9. Maintain information discipline.
10. Protect personal privacy.
11. All communication is public.
12. Operate as a team.

Media Guidelines

1. Always welcome and assist.
2. Never say no comment.
3. Demonstrate empathy and concern.
4. Never speculate or blame.
5. Stick with approved information.
6. Never stray from your own area of responsibility.
7. Every question is a chance to repeat key messages.
8. Never turn your back on a camera.
9. How you say it is more important than what you say.
10. Keep it brief and to the point.
11. Monitor and respond quickly to rumors, misinformation, misleading reporting.

Stakeholder Guidelines

1. Your future lies in their trust in you--never compromise that trust.
2. Prioritize based on their impact on your future and their influence over others.
3. Communicate directly with them.
4. Never allow them to find out critical info through the media.
5. Respond to questions, comments and suggestions quickly and positively.
6. Respond to rumors, misinformation and emerging issues quickly.
7. Personal meetings and phone conversations important with key stakeholders.
8. Communication serves as conduit between leadership and stakeholders.

Table of Contents

Introduction

Complicated and Simple Plans

The "Playbook" Model

Where this Plan Came From

Crisis plans are too simple.
And too complicated.

Crisis plans are both too complicated and too simple. So the "One Page Crisis Communication Playbook" attempts to solve both those problems at once.

They are usually too complicated because they come in big binders, red sometimes, with lots of pages. The problem, or course, is that when the big one hits there are very few who are going to take the time to read the manual or sift through all the pages to find the nuggets of information they need. This crisis communication plan solves that by putting all essentials on a single page in graphic form to be used as a simple guide for both training and managing real events.

They are too simple for several reasons.

Too media centric

One, they are typically focused on media management which concentrates most if not all effort on carefully crafting messages to be put into press releases or talking points for press conferences. The world has moved on. We live in a post-media world with multiple channels and many new factors influencing public opinion. Public participation is now the name of the game. Current crisis communication plans take into account direct communication and interaction with many important audiences, the media being one of them. This plan is based on the belief that the most important communication occurs between you and those people whose opinion about you matters most for your future. To execute on that "direct interaction" strategy, you must be the "broadcaster." You must be your own channel for the most up-to-date, relevant and credible information about the event.

They don't scale

Two, they don't scale. Recent events have shown that when it comes to planning you can't think big enough. You don't want a plan that works for small to mid-size events and then have a big kerfluffle happen that is way too big for your plans. An effective plan works for the smallest events and scales up to work effectively for events bigger than you ever thought possible—because that is what is needed in a time of mega-crises.

Not experience-based

Third, they're not based on real life experience. Too often communication leaders try to run a crisis communication operation just like they run their normal, daily activities—just faster and bigger. There is a situation where that is appropriate and we'll talk about that near the end of this playbook. But for most organizations today, trying to simply step up what you are doing every day when the world is crashing around you is a recipe for failure. The plan included here is based on the most tried and true communication processes and structures used by professional communicators over the past twenty some years. It works.

Why a "Playbook?"

In this plan template I've used the term "playbook" as an analogy. My apologies to those who are not American football fans. The model here is the method used by coaches to place an entire game plan with multiple plays into a document that fits over the forearm or wrist of the quarterback. That plan with a few notations contains everything needed by the quarterback to make the right calls to direct a team of eleven players to victory. Of course, there is far more to the playbook than what fits on the quarterback's wrist. There are the years of experience and planning poured into a manual that details the moves of every one of the eleven players. The plays envision a multitude of different scenarios or schemes that the defense may throw at them. It is a detailed creative exercise based on the best information available about what the team will face. The playbook is what is used for training. The wrist version used by the quarterback contains the short code that enables the team to respond quickly, effortlessly and effectively based on the practice with the playbook. The quarterback must call the plays, but for that to work the entire team must be very practiced in those plays and no exactly what the quarterback is talking about. Without the wrist version and without the complete playbook behind it, chaos may soon follow.

That is what is envisioned here. This manual is the playbook behind the One Page Guide. It is intended to be used for training and preparation. Perhaps someone will get this manual out during a real event. If so, it is probably because the moves have not yet become instinctive. Or more likely, new members have been added to the team during an event and they need to understand how the game is being played. If the team is well prepared and knows the plays inside out, the only thing needed during the response will be the One Page—and then just as a reminder and check list. And a good quarterback calling the right plays.

Where this plan came from

At the risk of making your eyes cross with jargon and alphabet soup before you even get out of this Introduction, I need to tell you where the core ideas of this plan came from. I got involved in the whole large-scale disaster and crisis management business in 1999 through the Olympic Pipeline accident in my hometown. Since then, I have worked with several hundred government agencies from the federal to the small town level, as well as most of the global oil companies operating in the US. I've also worked with hospitals, universities, non-profit agencies—both domestic and global, and a variety of companies in the food, aircraft manufacturing, financial services and many other different lines of business.

That pipeline accident was my introduction to the Incident Command System—the response plan used at that time by the Coast Guard, other government agencies and oil companies in the wake of the ExxonValdez disaster in 1989. In 2004 the Incident Command System (ICS—I'll just go ahead and start with the alpha-soup and jargon) has been adopted as part of the National Incident Management System (NIMS—there we go again). Under President George W. Bush it was mandated for use by all government agencies at all levels—with the threat being loss of federal funding if they didn't comply.

Users of the Incident Command System, particularly the Coast Guard, evolved a management protocol for media and public communication called the Joint Information Center (get ready—the JIC, pronounced "jick"). The meat of the One Page plan is the underlying structure of the JIC.

Why base this on the JIC model? Because it works. And, because many crises or events will involve a coordinated response, often with government agencies including local police, fire departments or emergency management operations. They play by these rules (often, I should say, because despite the years of pushing there is still much uneven use). If you find yourself needing to work with them, it helps a lot to know the rules of the game as they play it and maybe even understand a little of the jargon they are talking. (A glossary is included in this manual to help you wade through it if you find yourself in the middle of alpha soup talking response-types.)

The basic JIC structure works in large events (like the 2010 gulf spill where it was used effectively in the early stages until politics intervened). It also works great in small events, because it follows naturally what I call the communication cycle. This is the normal process we go through to communicate so it will most likely make perfect sense to you and seem overly obvious. The problem is in a big crisis, suddenly you may be working with a rapidly expanding team, many of whom are perfect strangers, and now you have to get organized to work together to accomplish something that you do every day and can do with your eyes closed while falling off a chair. That's why crisis communications gets complicated, and why it is not as easy as it looks to make it look easy as it looks.

Phase 1: Notifications

Notification Summary

Event Occurs

Initial Notifications

Initial Information Gathering

Initial Assessment

Notification Summary   Something bad happens. You get a call with the barest of details. You try to find out as much as you can so you can tell just how bad this is. Perhaps the media are already calling. Perhaps that is how you found out about it in the first place and you said to the reporter, "I'll get back to you." You know you need to start communicating or the game will be lost before you even get out of the gate. It's pretty certain social media is already trending hot and it's not going to be pretty. ("Trending hot" is a reference to those social media monitoring sites that track the keywords appearing in social media channels like Twitter. Results are often shown in a "word cloud" with the biggest words appearing the most often.) You know by now that you are not going to be able to handle this alone. Fact is, you can't even handle what you have in front of you right now alone. So you have to get your team assembled, organized, and put to work. All while trying to answer the questions that are now flooding in, with the barest of information you have.

That, in summary, is the notification process.

Now, let's formalize it a bit and add in some important details and decisions.

Event Occurs

This plan is intended to address almost every kind of crisis or emergency. But the range of events which might be considered crises or emergencies is very big. For the sake of trying to simplify, let's define a crisis or emergency this way:

Defining a crisis

- It happens quickly and requires urgent response
- It impacts or threatens some really important things, like:
  - People's health or safety
  - People's future well-being (like financial security)
  - The environment, community, animals or the building you are in
  - You, your co-workers, or the entire organization's future

Defining a crisis with a nailed-down definition is a little like art. In fact, it is like art in that most people may not be able to explain it, but they know a crisis when they see it. Still, it is important to be able to say what is a crisis and what it is not and to be able to classify it in some way in order to guide the response and decide how big of a team and who you really need on your team. That is covered under Phase 3: Assessment.

Smoldering crises and gray swans

I said that a crisis is something that happens quickly. The truth is, a great many crises come with a lot of warning. Some estimates are that as many as 75% of crises are "smoldering"—there is smoke but no fire. That is true of a great many business crises such product recalls, legal issues, and labor issues. But it is also true of certain natural disasters such as severe storms, flooding, even volcanoes. Some are true "black swans" that appear to come out of nowhere—but even a number of those, such as the financial crisis that affected our world in the past few years can be seen in retrospect to be quite predictable. Hindsight tends to make sudden events look remarkably likely.

Types of crises

One of the most effective means of dealing with crises is to identify the smoke and deal with that before it turns into fire. That takes courage and the courage needed in many large organizations to address the smoldering crises, sometimes called the elephants in the room, is often missing. That's an organizational culture issue and beyond what I should be dealing with here.

What is crucial here is that not all crises come like a thief in the night. There are things we might call "gray swans," that do not completely appear out of nowhere, yet adequate preparation has not been made for them. As a crisis communication manager, you should know that the gray swans, as well as smoldering crises are particularly dangerous because if it can be shown that your organization knew something, or could have known something, but ignored it, well, it's going to make matters worse.

All good crisis plans have a list of crisis events which the plan is intended to cover. I suggest you make that list and its one tasks I can't help you with through this manual, only because I have to be broad enough to cover a wide range of events. However, I have adopted a list of crisis events that are fairly broad organized into three main causes. The cause is important because there is a vast difference in approach whether or not your organization caused the event, or you are merely responding to something caused by others or even an "act of God."

Three basic crisis categories

The three categories are:

Natural Disasters (Act of God sorts of things)

External Caused (Someone did it, but you didn't)

Internal Caused (Oops, you did it)

The following is not intended to be a complete list, but some representative kinds of crises and events for you to use as a guide in developing a list of major events that could impact your organization.

Natural Disasters

Tropical Storm/Hurricane

Tsunami

Earthquake

Flooding

External Caused

Major Accident—Non-Company related

Terrorist Attack/Criminal Activity

Suspicious Package or Mail

Security Breach

Activist Physical Attack with Damage, Injuries or Fatalities

Pandemic

Activist/Competitor/NGO Public Accusations

Legal Action—Class Action

Internal Caused

Employee Accident—No public impact

Accident—public impact

Explosion-Fire

Environmental Release (non oil spill)

Labor Issue

Management Misdeeds

Sexual Assault or Harassment

Management Loss

Product Safety Issue

Major customer or financial loss

Government investigation

As you can see, this isn't a perfectly neat list either. Included in "Internal Caused" are explosions or fires—but they could be in "External Caused" as well. There are a number of other examples of gray areas (Government Investigation?), but this should help in both coming up with your own nightmares and understanding that the differences in cause makes a difference in communications.

Risk Matrix

A very helpful tool in preparing to respond to crises is the risk matrix. Here's what a Risk Matrix looks like:

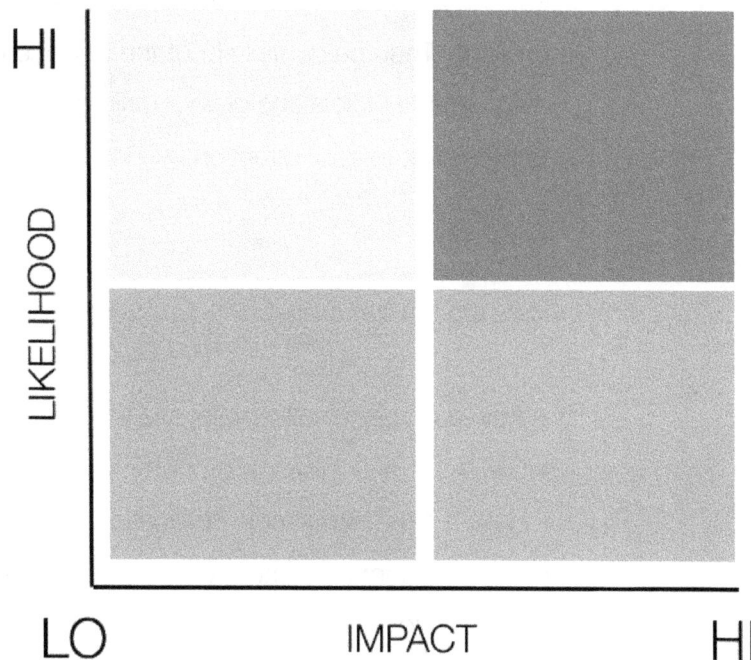

HI

LIKELIHOOD

LO   IMPACT   HI

By plotting your crisis scenarios on the matrix, you can quite easily prioritize your preparation efforts. Clearly, it makes more sense to focus on those events in the Red Zone, the ones both most likely to occur and with the most impact, than on the events in the Green Zone.

Walking your senior leadership team through a Risk Matrix exercise is one of the most valuable things you can do for your organization. It helps focus everyone on the potential crisis scenarios, helps bring to light the potential smoldering crises, and reveals the concerns that senior management may have about those things that cause the most worry.

One big caution, and I hate to have to say this. Recent events have demonstrated that some attorneys will make use of this kind of preparation material in lawsuits against the company. Instead of demonstrating that this kind of exercise represents prudent preparation, it will be presented as: "See, they knew this was a danger, even ranked it as one of their main concerns, and then did not prepare adequately for it." If this is a concern and it perhaps should be, my advice is to consult with your crisis attorney and consider having the attorney participate in this process so that the entire exercise and documentation may be covered under attorney client privilege. Then be careful about the trail of emails, conversations and other discoverable indications of your deliberations and conclusions. Sad I have to bring that to your attention.

Caution in identifying risks

Here are the basic rules:

- Train and prepare all employees who may be first to spot a problem
- Call 9-1-1 first if lives or property are in immediate danger
- Have a clear and simple notification process for your crisis response team
- The lead communicator needs to be on the initial contact list
- Use multiple means of notifying—phone (multiple numbers), text, email

- Have backup for key positions – best to have all major positions covered by three or more trained employees
- Train employees in your "refer and defer" policies

Initial Notifications

The good thing about starting first thinking about events that may happen is that you can identify who will likely be the first to notice and identify it as a problem, maybe a big problem. For example, for a food processing company, a food safety issue may be first detected in the lab, in quality control, or maybe through a customer call center. For an oil refinery, dock or terminal workers involved in transferring crude from ships or pipelines may be the first to spot a developing spill. Whoever is on the "front line," on the scene, or at an early warning stage must be part of your crisis response plan. They need to know who to call and what the notification process is.

Train and prepare employees who may be first to notice

The health of your entire organization may depend on early detection. Make certain the sensors are in place. The people who may be there to spot the problem need to know what problems may emerge and need to have very clear information about what to do.

Call 9-1-1 if immediate danger

Of course, if lives are endangered the first call must be to 9-1-1.

Simple initial notification

But who do they call after that? It must be instinctive and clear to them. There should be no more than three names or numbers on the initial call list for any unit or employee group. Some larger organizations have an easily remembered 800 number. The numbers to call should be distributed broadly, particularly in areas where events may first be experienced, or provided in wallet cards or other very portable and easily accessed forms.

After the initial call, a more detailed notification call list may be used by the people or office receiving the initial notification.

Communications—be one of the first

As the communication lead for the organization, you must be very early in the call process. Your organization may have (should have) a crisis response team and the lead public affairs person for the organization or a designated crisis communication lead needs to be one of first to be notified.

Use multiple means of notifying

The phones may not be working. The first to go will be landlines—home and office phones. Cell phones are more resilient than landlines particularly if there are power outages. However, if a big event happens—big storm, earthquake, attack—the cell phone system will be overwhelmed very quickly as everyone tries to use it. Text messages work on the same cell network, but use data channels instead of voice channels and so are much more resilient. Data channels can carry much more traffic.

You must prepare to use several different methods to reach those who need to respond. For certain high-risk organizations where much is at stake, it is not too much to consider satellite phones as a more fool-proof means of notifying.

Backup for key positions

For each of the key positions on a response team there should be at least three available to fill that role. That includes the communication lead. That's a problem for many organizations who don't have that depth, but if you don't you may want to consider an outside contractor with the experience and qualifications needed. To leave the initial notifications going to a single person puts the organization at considerable risk if that person can't be reached.

Train employees how to refer media to spokespersons

The traditional crisis communications rules said only authorized spokespersons should speak to the media. However, the media will often turn an employees deflection of questions into a perceived attempt by the company to control the message (which it is, but which the media equate to lack of transparency). As a result, you need to be very careful about policies that say only authorized spokespersons should speak to the media. An appropriate policy today is to let employees know that they are all free to speak to the media but are restricted to their own area of responsibility. They can talk specifically about their role and what they do, but not speak on behalf of any other area or the company as a whole. And they need to make that clear to the media if asked. Employee training should include how they can communicate their willingness to help the reporter get the information they need, how to help identify the spokesperson, and how to politely and firmly refuse the often stubborn attempts to get an authorized quotation or emotional reaction.

Initial Information Gathering

Now you play reporter. It is your job to get the key facts as quickly as possible. There are two things you need to do with those facts. One, make an initial assessment. How bad is this? How much worse could it get? Two, who most urgently needs to know what about this event?

Because we live in a time of instant news, information about an event travels at the speed of light around the world through the Internet. We no longer are dependent on news reporters with big printing presses and millions of dollars of broadcast equipment to get information about something that is important or interesting to us. We can get it instantly from anyone who has information about it. This means that if the event you are involved in is at all visible to anyone either inside or outside your organization, you will likely start to get questions about the same time as you get your first notification. If you are a designated communication person for your organization, you may get calls from the media or others even BEFORE you get your call to activate.

Instant News

Here's the dilemma in this instant news situation we are trying to maneuver:

- You have almost immediate demands to communicate about the event.
- You also have to have time to activate your team, get everyone organized and get the information machine running.
- The "facts" you get about the initial response may very well be wrong and getting approved "facts" to communicate is very difficult while everyone is gearing up.
- If you get something quite wrong (like how much oil is in water) you will be torn apart and might never recover—this is particularly true if the message is seen to minimize impacts in any way.
- Conversely, raising alarm unnecessarily is also a potential career-ender.
- If you say nothing, or are slow to respond, it is hard to avoid looking inept, inadvertently communicating that the response team is disorganized, or communicating that your organization is ignorant or oblivious to the situation.

It's a tough spot. But the strategy here is to prepare as much in advance as possible so you can make an initial statement that communicates you are on top of things. With the publishing of that statement you will give yourself some time to assemble your team while not appearing to go incognito.

Questions to ask

Who, what, when, where, how, why--all those reporter questions. But in these first precious minutes you have to focus on what is really important:

- what happened?

- Are there injuries, fatalities?

- Is anyone in immediate danger? (If so, the first priority is to prepare warnings or directions for those who may be impacted to reduce the risk, such as evacuation, shelter-in-place, boil water, etc.)

- What is being done right now to respond?

- Could this get worse and if so, how? (If there is the potential for this quickly evolving into something that could put safety, health or the environment at risk, it must be determined what messages need to be prepared now and whether or not to distribute.)

- Who has been notified, who is responding, what resources are being deployed?

That's about all that is needed for the initial information. We'll get into more details about the message and distribution later. You may notice some questions that are missing:

- How did this happen?

- Why did it happen?

- Who is to blame?

- How big is the problem?

Topics to avoid

Those are questions that you may be curious about and certainly news reporters and many citizens will want to know about very quickly. You may even know what the answers are. But there are three basic rules to follow in this very initial stage of providing information:

- Don't deny the obvious.

- Don't speculate.

- Don't minimize.

If the cause of the emergency is plain for everyone to see then it makes no sense to avoid the obvious questions about cause. ("The cause of the building collapse is under investigation" when everyone knows the earth shook.) At the same time, some of the worst public information mistakes are made when early information about what caused the problem turns out to be wrong. Either way, credibility is lost. Stick to the clear, indisputable or verified and approved facts from the response leader.

Dealing with cause

Reporters are trained to try and find cause very early, particularly when there the public or innocents are harmed. You may have a pretty good idea but it may turn out to be wrong and that will cause many problems later. You may understand at this point that it is not your company or organization's fault and point fingers at someone else. That may lead to mutual finger pointing and if mistakes are made, a high price will be paid later. So, unless the cause is fully and completely known or obvious, it is almost always better to defer those questions. Reporters will work hard to get you to speculate: "I understand you don't KNOW what caused it, but what do you THINK caused it?" Don't go there.

Never minimize

It is natural to want to minimize the event and the damage or harm it has caused. And you may be right about the limitation at that moment. But, if it turns out to be bigger than first thought, your and your organization's credibility will be severely attacked. Everything you say after that will be put under the cloud of minimizing. At the same time, you don't want to create a bigger event than exists or cause unnecessary fear and uncertainty or draw any more attention than is already there. Finding that fine line is why good crisis communication leaders get the big bucks.

While the process of assessing the event for the purpose of calling out the necessary communication team is covered in Phase 3, you will not be able to avoid doing an initial assessment. So, go ahead and do it. Just how bad is this now? What direction is it heading? Is it going to get worse? How much worse could it get? What else might occur, related or unrelated, that would really complicate things?

This initial assessment is important in putting into place the steps you have prepared. Should the initial message be simply published on a website? Should it be sent to everyone on your list? Who should be notified right now? How big of a team might be needed to respond? All these things will be going through your head. Proper preparation means you have considered these eventualities and have organized responses into certain buckets or categories. Now you have to match up the facts on the ground with the different categories or scales of response you have thought through and prepared for.

One of the reasons to do an initial assessment at this stage is for you as PIO or Communication Lead to get into a mind set of not just thinking about all the things you have to do right now, but be thinking ahead. Pilots are taught to "fly ahead of the airplane." You know when you are flying behind it and it's a dangerous thing. It is remarkably easy in a major event to start flying behind the airplane. Thinking ahead even at this early stage will help develop the important mental habit of staying ahead, preparing for the next stages even as you complete what is needed for this one.

Three assessment questions

With that in mind, you need to think about answering three questions in this initial assessment.

1. How bad is it right now?

How will you answer the question about how bad it really is to the first person you talk to? You say: "Such and such happened." They say: "How bad is it?" You say, "Well, pretty bad." Doesn't really work, does it? That's why most crisis plans identify different levels of event so they can plan for a response scaled to the event. Some use colors: Green, Yellow, Red. Some use numbers: Level 1, Level 2, Level 3. Some use Roman numerals: I, II, III. You might notice I'm only using three levels. I've worked with plans that have clearly identified seven levels and that's just too many. Keep it simple. That's why I prefer the color coding. It avoids explaining what your code means. Effective planning helps you save time when you need it most and you don't want to spend a lot of time when things are hitting the fan explaining just how far the stuff is flying. Try to define in simple clear terms just what the colors mean, for example:

Green – we wish this wouldn't have happened but looks like it can be handled with minimal damage or impact. But it's important to monitor to see it doesn't get worse.

Orange – this is going to cause some serious damage or impact and may hurt us for some time. But it is not the "big one" with widespread destruction including to our future.

Red – this is the big one. All hands on deck. But, just because it's big doesn't mean it can't get bigger or worse.

2. How bad could it get?

Don't make the mistake of thinking that what you are presented with right now is what you will have to deal with. Things have a tendency of piling on. Bad things come in threes and sometimes a lot more than that. It may get worse just because the initial information about an event is almost always wrong. But it may get worse because whatever went wrong can cause other things to go wrong. Sometimes, it gets worse because the media and public interest in one event leads to questions and increased scrutiny about other things that suddenly become relevant. So, when presented with the initial information just be aware that your world is suddenly quite unstable and you need to prepare for that.

3. What do we do now to respond as well as prepare for the worst?

Since your job is communicating, the actions you need to put in place are about getting information out about the event to those who will have a lot of interest in it—the media, the public, government leaders, employees, community members, on and on. Calls may be coming in already and if the event is visible, social media will already be buzzing. Now you need to divide your mind in two and get going on putting into action the plans you had prepared for quickly getting the important event information out—usually the Initial Statement or Message. But you also have to keep one eye out for preparations that may need to be put in place in case things really do get bad. To use the pilot analogy, you need to get this communication plane off the ground and while you are taxiing onto the active runway, be thinking well ahead of the airplane as to what you may encounter when you're rolling down the runway and climbing out.

Phase 2: Initial Message

Be fast or be irrelevant
Initial statement templates
Pre-approvals
The human element
The simple, important facts
Setting expectations
Choosing channels

Be fast or be irrelevant

You may be surprised, stunned even, to see that the first thing to do is get an initial message out. That is simply not the way crisis communication plans have been built in the past. But we don't ride around on horses anymore and we don't have time to wait for the news satellite trucks to show up before we need to start communicating. The change is the Internet and the way it connects the majority of people on earth in a vast network that enables us to communicate with each other anywhere at the speed of light. We can't hang around here right now to talk about how the Internet in general and social media in particular has transformed how the public gets informed about almost any event. But if you are not aware or convinced yet that news about just about any crisis involving you and your company will be told first on the Internet and social media and from there spread almost instantaneously to major media outlets and anyone else with a strong interest, then I suggest you put this plan down and pick up some of the hundreds of articles, books and blog sites talking about this remarkable transformation.

The reason getting an initial message out about your event is so important is because if you don't you and your organization will look completely out of touch with reality. At the very minimum you must communicate that you are aware of what everyone is talking about and will provide additional information very soon. Don't misunderstand me. It is very unlikely that any information you provide will be the first that people will find out about whatever the crisis is. It can happen, but only when it is so secure behind closed doors that even family members of employees involved who use Facebook, Twitter, Tumblr or blog sites don't know anything about what is happening. The number of crises in the highly secure and confined category seems to keep diminishing. Which means that others are going to be communicating about "your" crisis probably well before you can get your crisis communication machine started, and maybe even before you find out about it.

Initial statement templates

As with most things that need to be done in a big hurry, the more prepared you are the more easily you can respond with the necessary speed. When things start moving fast after a sudden and explosive event occurs, you will find yourself trying to do three primary things at once:

1) answer questions from the media, executives, employees, etc.,

2) get a statement out that shows you are on it, and

3) get your team assembled so you can start digging out the hole that trying to do 1 and 2 is causing.

So, how do you do it? Have a number of initial statement templates prepared in advance. Get them pre-approved (see next point), and get them published or sent (see "Choosing channels" below).

Initial statement content

What does an initial statement say? There are usually four essential elements:

1) a very brief statement of what is happening or has happened

2) if appropriate, an expression of empathy and concern for those affected

3) a brief statement about what is being done to respond to the incident

4) a commitment to provide additional information in the very near future and guidance on where to find that.

In other words, something like this:

"XYZ Corporation confirms that an accident has occurred at the Blueberry Point facility located at 1313 Undine Avenue and that injuries have been reported. We deeply regret that this accident happened and that our valued employees have been injured. All appropriate response authorities have been notified and our emergency response team has been activated and is working closely with emergency responders. The cause of this accident is under investigation. We will provide additional information about this event as soon as it becomes available on our incident website at www.xyzcorpresponds.com."

Sure, it's not a lot, doesn't provide the details people are looking for at this stage. But, if you delay to confirm a lot of details and get the necessary approvals, then it will likely slow you down. And during that "quiet period" the social media channels are going nuts, media reports are ramping up, those most interested are going to your website and finding…what? Nothing. Like you are oblivious. So it is much better to get the sketchy available information out there so you and your team can get to work to provide the facts and information that everyone will be looking for.

There's one more reason to focus on that initial statement as your first priority. Above I said you are trying to do three things, the first being answer questions—from the media and almost everyone else. Trouble is, if you stop to answer those, you'll never get that statement out. So getting that statement out quickly allows you to say to those who are calling, "We have published the information we have available on our website at (address). You can sign up there for updates or keep checking that site as we will put available information there first."

That message does a couple of things. It communicates that you are communicating. You are not hiding, not stonewalling, not oblivious. It buys you time as you don't have to tell the story and take the time to answer a bunch of the same questions. It, perhaps most importantly, tells them where they can get the best information which is on your website. This will have the result of dramatically, yes I mean dramatically, cutting down on the number of calls you have to answer. Much more on that later.

Pre-approvals

If your organization's policy is to have multiple people approve any message before it can be sent, I have to say you are probably doomed before you begin. Particularly if that policy applies to your initial message. If you need to get legal, HR, investor relations, the CEO, the CEO's assistant and several others with C's in their titles, you are simply not going to be able to get that message out in a way that accomplishes what we are trying to do. Information approvals are important, and they are a fact of life for practically any communicator facing crisis events, but they are also a prime reason for the pundits standing around after a reputation funeral to shake their heads and say "too little, too late."

The initial statement templates should all be pre-approved. Likely with that agreement you will need to agree to stay completely within the template and only add the relevant information. If pre-approvals cannot be provided, keep working the templates until you get the pre-approvals. If that is simply not possible, it's time to talk to the higher authorities (in your organization I mean) about why speed is essential today.

Empathy: the human element

You will note the second essential element of the template we discussed above is a statement of care or empathy. We have Dr. Vincent Covello largely to thank for bringing this all-important human element to the forefront of risk and crisis communication. As he teaches: "they won't care what you know until they know that you care." Some of the biggest reputation problems in crisis events have been caused by statements that indicated a minimizing of the impact or suggest that the organization's focus or concern was other than how the event they caused was hurting others. The more your event is your fault and the greater its impact on those who are innocent bystanders, the greater the importance of expressing and demonstrating concern for those whose lives, health, safety or future has been harmed by what you have caused.

There are several problems with empathy statements that have to be considered when developing them. First, legal issues may arise when a statement is understood to accept a level of responsibility that may cause problems in court. This is a very difficult and sensitive area because saying you are sorry when you have caused problems is one of the most important tenets of crisis communication. The only way to manage this is to work it out in advance and help senior leaders to understand the importance of statements of responsibility and regret. Second, these statements have

27

become a common part of crisis management and so have lost impact but their use. "We deeply regret the impact this event has caused..." just doesn't carry the same weight as it has become almost cliché. The solution is to find meaningful ways of communicating concern, which leads to the third point: actions speak louder than words. While this initial statement may be too early to describe actions the organization is taking that demonstrates real concern, if you have that, use it. If you are in a position to say, for example, that the company has sent teams of employees to personally assess damage and work with families who have been harmed, that goes much further than simply saying we care.

The simple, important facts

Using an initial statement template will force you to stick to a few basic facts. The primary purpose of it is to recognize and confirm that an event has taken place, then give yourself and your team time to get the wheels of the crisis communication operation moving. The temptation will be to add more details than the basic facts. Of course, if there are confirmed details that are obvious or widely known, and getting approval to add them does not slow you down too much, they should be added. But otherwise resist the temptation to try to turn the initial statement into a full-blown information release.

Setting expectations

In addition to letting the media, the public and your stakeholders know that an incident is going on, one other important purpose of the initial statement is to let them know when they can expect additional information. If you have a crisis dark site and that will be launched with a different web address or url, then direct their attention there. If you know when you will put out an update or a major information release, go ahead and announce that but then make sure you do it. In general, it is fine to say "we will provide additional information as it becomes available," even though that is far weaker than being more specific. The point is to set expectations about upcoming communication—then meet or exceed those expectations.

Choosing channels

We will save a more in-depth discussion about communication channels to use for the Workflow section, specifically when talking about Information Dissemination. However, the initial statement needs to be available to those seeking it and in some cases, needs to be distributed to reporters and stakeholders. The basic options today are:

- your organization's primary website
- a crisis or emergency website
- email distributions
- text distributions
- your organization's Twitter account
- your organization's FaceBook page (and/or your Google+ page)

This is a continually moving target and by the time I write this and you read it, the landscape may have changed. So we'll stick to the basics: where is your audience? Where will they expect to find information from you? Is it sufficient to publish something in a fairly discreet manner, or is it in your interest to broadcast the message far and wide (see discussion on reactive vs. proactive strategy under Assessment)?

Like most other decisions at this time, you don't want to have to really think this through when all heck is breaking loose. Think about it in advance. Relate it to the types and levels of incidences you may face. Develop your contact lists, your methods of providing immediate content to the appropriate websites, and choose the best channels to use. Then make certain that all of it is ready for you to use from wherever and whenever.

Phase 3: Assessment

Event types and resources needed
Reactive vs. Proactive Strategies
Setting Triggers

**Event types and
resources needed**

So the event happens, you find out about it (notification), you get a message prepared or sent out saying "Yes, something is going on" (initial message). Now you have to determine just how bad it is and how much help you are going to need to get through this (assessment).

If you did your job making a list of potential crisis events and put them on a risk matrix, you did much of the pre-work of assessment. You now have a good idea of the risks, the likelihood, the potential impact and the potential scope or size of these events. There are two main reasons to go thoughtfully through this stage of assessment:

1) to activate the team you need to effectively respond
2) to apply the appropriate communication strategy given the event unfolding

There almost as many different ways of categorizing event levels as there are crisis plans. I've seen plans with as many as seven distinct levels, many have five, but I prefer three. And I like to color code them for simplicity and ease of communication:

Green = Low Level

Yellow = Mid Level

Red = High Level

It should be noted that these don't correspond to the quadrants in the risk matrix. Rather they are used to aid in calling out the team and determining initial response communication strategy. We'll talk about calling out the appropriate team in the next section. So let's talk about strategy.

Reactive vs proactive

Here is where we run into one of the biggest challenges in crisis communication.

Should we merely respond to the emergence of the story, or should we try and get ahead of it? Should we wait and see how big it is going to get, or should we make some assumptions and run the risk that we fan the flames of media and public interest? Should we remain reactive or move into proactive communications? There are few areas in crisis communication where good judgment, experience and the right relationship with senior executives are more important.

Serious mistakes have been made in both directions. Too much caution out of fear of elevating a story that otherwise would have had minimal interest and there is the very real likelihood that whatever you do will be too little, too late. The Book of Samurai says: "When there is something to be said, it is better if it is said right away. If it is said later, it will sound like an excuse." The recent history of reputation crises most often carry the post-mortem comment of too little, too late. So, I would say on balance, more reputation damaging mistakes are made erring on the side of caution.

However, it is likely that more public relations and crisis communications careers may be lost by the hindsight that shows actions taken heightened the story. No communication manager wants to be accused of creating a negative story, or of elevating one by the advice given or actions taken.

There are three answers to this dilemma I'd like to suggest There are three answers to this dilemma I'd like to suggest as part of your plan:

- Use three options, not two: Reactive, Semi-Proactive and Proactive
- Pre-set triggers
- Include a veteran crisis communication advisor on your team

Three Response Strategy Options

Reactive Strategy

The first option, reactive, normally consists of creating a holding statement or standby statement. These are prepared in anticipation of questions that may be asked should the event come to the attention of the media, stakeholders, employees or anyone outside the small circle trying to manage and contain the event. Creating such a statement is essential for any event where questions may emerge.

Semi-proactive

The second option I'm calling semi-proactive. It involves publishing a statement about the event on the organization's website or newsroom site. It can be published in a fairly inconspicuous location, but making it too inconspicuous defeats one of the main purposes of this. What makes this semi-proactive is that it does not involve distribution of the message— merely publishing. The benefits of doing this are primarily in being transparent and providing an easy way to answer questions should they arise. When you get a call or email from a reporter, investor or key stakeholder, you can simply refer them to the statement on the website letting them know that you published information on this topic earlier. That makes it clear you are not hiding or trying to diminish the event. Of course, this carries the risk that the information will be picked up and spread via Internet to others including the media resulting in the publication elevating the story. That's why this approach should be used when it is very likely that questions will emerge and when the cost of appearing to be hiding, covering up or non-transparent is significant. But, it follows the well established dictum in crisis management that bad news about you should come from you rather from those whose agenda may not be positive toward you.

Proactive Distribution

The third option is publishing the statement plus distributing and seeking wide distribution. This is the appropriate course when it is very clear that the story will receive wide-spread coverage and it is to your advantage to participate early in the telling of the story. Note that in the semi-proactive option I did not suggest publishing this on your Twitter account or Facebook page or other social media channels you may use. The reason for that is these channels are distribution channels and not merely publishing. They are intended to "push" information out to others who subscribe and make it exceptionally easy for others to further distribute the information. For proactive distribution, the social media channels, in addition to your own pre-staged media and stakeholder email lists, are the most important way of getting information out on a broad bases—including to the media.

Setting Triggers

One advantage of color-coding events is you can use them to help set initial strategy as well. In general, and I emphasize in general because events rarely fit into the neat categories established during planning. But, in general, you can set the strategy triggers like this:

Green = Holding Statement—reactive strategy

Yellow = Initial statement published on website – semi-proactive strategy

Red = Initial statement widely distributed, website, email lists, social media channels

This does bring some nice consistency between the strategy employed and the size of the team you need. A small team is needed if holding statements are only used. If the event unfolds where more open communication is advised, the event is reassessed to a Yellow and the Yellow team activated along with publication on the website. And a Red event, whether evolving or suddenly upon you, requires maximum distribution and a maximum team to deal with the questions and on-going information flow implied in such an event.

It still leaves the question about the basis of setting the triggers. How do you know when to determine Green, Yellow or Red? When to implement reactive, semi-proactive or proactive strategies? Nearly every organization is going to view this question differently—indeed, how much transparency an organization's leaders are comfortable with is a distinct sign of the corporate culture. Here is a basic chart you can use as a starting point for setting your triggers or beginning the discussion about where those triggers should be set:

Levels	Impact on Organization	Media, Stakeholder or Public Interest	Communication Strategy
Green	Minor if at all	No media, some stakeholder interest	No public communication, very targeted and limited stakeholder communication. Prepare holding statement.
Green-2		Limited media and public interested, moderate stakeholder	Holding statement used for media & public inquiries. Targeted stakeholder communication
Yellow	Minor to Moderate	No media or public interest, but high stakeholder interest	Holding statement, no public message on website. More aggressive direct messaging to stakeholders.
		Moderate media and public interest, moderate to high stakeholder interest	Publish limited statement on website. Prepare Q&A or Fact Sheets for possible release. Aggressive direct messages to stakeholders.
Red	Major to potentially fatal impact	High regional, national or global media and public interest	Proactive distribution—limit to regional if interest is regional, same for national. Global interest—widest possible distribution

Phase 4: Team Activation

Event levels and teams

Expanded resources

Activation methods

Matching resources to scale of event

Your pre-planning at this stage consists of matching up the communication resources you need to the scale or scope of the event. I like to use the three event levels to identify scale and I like to assign colors to them:

Green = low level

Yellow = mid-level

Red = high level

Then it is easy to identify the members of your team by colors. You have the Green Team, the Yellow Team and the Red Team.

The problem is, as always, it is not quite as simple as this. Different types of events may require different skill sets and different resources. For example, some events may involve a high level of community impact and engagement but relatively moderate media engagement. But, you can also have events with lots of media attention but that don't require an extensive team to work with community members or groups or government folks. There are likely other subdivisions based on the kind of organization you are and the kinds of events you face. With the objective of keeping it simple, your Red Team may have some sub-teams based on the specific needs of the event.

We'll have to wait until Phase 5 Communication Workflow to identify the specific skill sets and people you will need assigned to each team. The important thing here is to have readily available on a 24/7 basis the contact information for your teams. These can be prepared and organized on your smartphone or be web-based so you can access them at any time. For the larger events, it is advisable to use one of the many text/phone notification systems available, providing you can activate this from your smartphone.

Suggested teams

Levels	Impact on Organization	Media, Stakeholder or Public Interest	Team
Green	Minor if at all	No media, some stakeholder interest	Green 1 – smallest group
		Limited media and public interested, moderate stakeholder	Green 2 – additional support in stakeholder comms
Yellow	Minor to Moderate	No media or public interest, but high stakeholder interest	Yellow 1 – additional stakeholder comms
		Moderate media and public interest, moderate to high stakeholder interest	Yellow 2 – media specialists and stakeholder comms
Red	Major to potentially fatal impact	High regional media and public interest, high stakeholder	Red 1 – expanded team of media and stakeholder comms specialists
Red	Major to potentially fatal impact	High national or global media and public interest, maximum stakeholder	Red 2 – maximum team including expanded list of network or contractor support

Expanded resources

Your organization may not have risks that could translate into long-term global interest. Perhaps you are not a global oil company or a global brand. But please keep one thing in mind—when it comes to preparation it is almost impossible to think too big. Recent events from natural disasters to major environmental events to product recalls to food safety issues have demonstrated that thinking about how bad things can get is often too limited. As is understanding how many qualified people you will need if you find yourself the focus of the world's attention for any length of time. It is very difficult in the midst of a crisis to try to identify the people who you can call on for help. Now is the time to think bigger than you previously imagined and identify where you are going to get the people you need. I'm not saying you necessarily need to have a retainer agreement with a global PR firm, although that may help assure you of their responsiveness. What I am saying is to build a contact list of organizations and individuals that you can call on and have that readily available to you at all times. That means the list needs to be accessible by web or on your smartphone or both.

Activation methods

The methods of letting people know you need their help today range from the "hey you" method to sophisticated text and automated web-based notification systems. "Hey you" only works if your team is in the same office, in shouting distance, never on vacation or on an extended trip to the bathroom, and you can guarantee that you will never have an event during off hours.

Here is the range of methods of notifying your team and when it each method is advised:

"Hey You!"	Green 1 - 2	When your entire team is in shouting distance
Email	Green, Yellow and Red	When the situation is slowly evolving and urgent response not needed
Cell phone	Green, Yellow, Red	Most common method—takes too much time for team more than 4 or 5, fastest confirmation
Text	Yellow, Red	Much faster for larger team, best method if used with confirmation
2 way Text	Yellow, Red	Used to provide simplified confirmation of response
Automated phone	Red	Used to support text, redundancy, provides confirmation of receipt
All of the above	Red	Greatest assurance with confirmations

Unless you will always only have to call on a small team, some kind of automated text notification system is very important. Having this pre-staged with the contacts that were discussed above is also essential. Seconds count in those early minutes and hours of a response so you just don't have time to do all the leg work of finding who you need to contact and laboriously working through a list with a cell phone or land line. Your notification system should be web based or operate as an app to enable you to activate your team any hour of the day or night and no matter where you are located.

You also need to have multiple back-ups for accomplishing the activation. If you are the designated person and the only one with access to the list or notification tools, what happens if you are not reachable? No less than three people who are not likely to be in the same place at the same time when things happen (like on an airplane) need to be fully prepared to complete the activation.

Providing Directions   What will your message be to those people you are activating? "Help?!" A good start, but not enough. It's important to think through and prepare your activation message particularly since text is the primary means of notifying. Text messages are typically limited to 140 characters. You need to tell them:

- their services are urgently needed
- where they should report to (including if it is just to participate online using a web-based management system)
- whom they should report to
- how they should confirm

That's a lot to cover in 140 characters and it clearly suggests that some preparation and testing with your team is advised. The cryptic message you will be forced to send, and the means of confirming response, should be instantly understood and well practiced.

Confirmation

I've mentioned confirmation several times as part of activation. The reason is simple. You called out the team, but you don't know if they got the message, if they are on their way, if they are unreachable, if you need to start calling out replacements. You may end up trying them three or four times before deciding you need a replacement only to find out both of them are showing up now. That's a terrible waste of time. So build a confirmation process into whatever method you use to activate. If you are using a cell phone and you get voice mail, tell them to call you back as soon as they get this whether or not they are responding. If you are using text, include a way for them to text you back. Most notification systems include two-way texting means you can set up a means for them to text back and that will tell you all you need to know. Once this is set up they should be able to simply text "yes" or "no" to the designated text address and you will know what you need to know.

Phase 5: Communication Workflow

The Communication Cycle

Organization Structure

Scalability—Small and Large Organization Charts

Primary Roles Overview

A Smoothly Running Machine

Plan Operational Details

The Communication Cycle

Everything that has been done so far is designed to get us as quickly as possible to the point where the wheels of the communication machine can start going round and round, and the machine can begin producing the desired results.

If we think of the crisis communication workflow as a machine, then the components of the machine are people: your team. Whether they are a cohesive unit that has practiced their moves until they are automatic, or an ad hoc group consisting of individuals from different companies, agencies, public relations firms or long lost relatives, the success of the team depends on each person knowing their job and doing their job well.

The communication cycle is one of those things we do quite naturally as part of our daily lives without really thinking about it. Let's say someone in your family is suddenly taken to the hospital with a life-threatening condition. You have to get the word out to those who will care very much about this information. What do you do? First, you need to find out as accurately as you can exactly what is happening. What is the condition? What might be the cause? What suggests that it is as serious as it is? How was he or she taken to the hospital? What have you found out from the doctors so far? When do you expect to find out more? What is happening right now? What is the outlook? This is information gathering. If you try to communicate too quickly without any real facts, you may get it wrong with some pretty unhappy consequences. On the other hand, if you wait until you have the complete story before telling those who care, they will not be happy with you. Besides, the situation may have changed in the meantime and you'll be so busy catching up with the latest that you never get the word out. Those concerned will not be happy with you.

After you have gathered the information you need to figure out who is going to get it and exactly what you are going to say. Part of that is figuring out how you are going to reach them. Both the audience and the channels may change depending on who it is. Some might be best reached with a very brief text message. Some may need a phone call and the way you tell them about it may require some caution. For some, particularly those with strong interest but who may not be the closest family or friends, you may just want to get an informational message out as efficiently to as many at the same time as possible. This is what I'm calling Information Production.

After you've matched the messages to the audiences, then you need to actually get the word out. Phone calls, text messages, emails, whatever. Timing may be important. You don't want someone who is close to the one who is ill to complain because they heard about it in a roundabout way. This is called Information Dissemination.

Unless you are incredibly complete in your information and you have anticipated all possible questions and answered them in your message, your message will no doubt result in questions being asked. They will want more details about the illness, about how it happened, and probe for the limits of your knowledge on cause and prognosis. You are the information provider so you can't simply say you are too busy to answer. You must find out what the questions are, make sure you provide as complete information as you can, and learn from the questions what additional information you need to provide. This is called Inquiry Management.

For some of your important audiences, it will not be enough to get a text, a phone call or an email. There is something about us human beings that in times of great stress, fear or trouble, we want to get together with our loved ones, or others who are sharing our pain. You know when you send the message to your aging mother, for example, that she is going to need a visit real soon just to help her cope with the bad news. And to probe for further information. This is engagement.

In the process of getting questions, meeting together, sharing information you find out things from them. You find out what additional information they are looking for, but someone may say their uncle had a similar problem. You may also go to other sources, the Internet, or a doctor friend, to gather additional information about the illness. And you certainly will go back to the hospital, the ER, the doctors or whoever is closest to your ill family member to get the best information you can get. This is called Monitoring. It involves listening carefully to those asking questions, seeking additional information from outside and of course, getting additional information about the current status—which is what we called Information Gathering. It is largely the same process and tightly connected which is why we put Information Gathering and Monitoring in the same place on the wheel of the communication cycle.

Once you have secured additional information, you once again process it, decide who needs it, determine the best way to get it out, communicate it, deal with more questions, engage some more, monitor some more and round and round and round.

Here is the communication cycle as it appears in the One Page Playbook:

Info Gathering

Monitoring   **Info Production**

Engagement   **Dissemination**

Inquiry Management

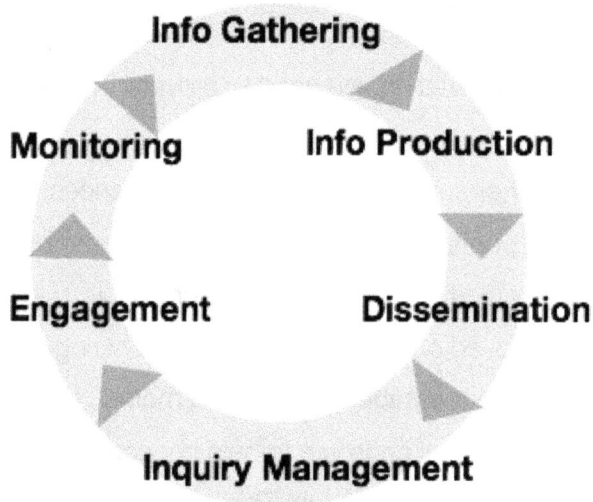

Organization Structure and Roles

You may be able to do all this for a seriously ill family member. But even then, you will be stretched and wish you had some help. If you did have help, you would start dividing up the responsibilities: "I'll call Aunt Marge while you check in with the hospital and see if there is anything new." Again, this is natural and normal, but can get a little complicated when the situation becomes more complex. Imagine then, if you find yourself as the information provider with audiences measuring in the hundreds, thousands or millions, and events rapidly unfolding in possibly many different locations, and with thousands, millions or billions of dollars of brand value, future employee income and ownership shares at stake. While the game must become elevated, it is very important to see that it is very much the same game. The communication cycle doesn't really change despite massive increases in scope and scale.

The bigger the scope and scale, the more critical it is to delegate properly— and that's what this section on Workflow is all about. You will see that we have stayed pretty close to the communication cycle in dividing up the work.

Here is the organization chart from the One Page Playbook:

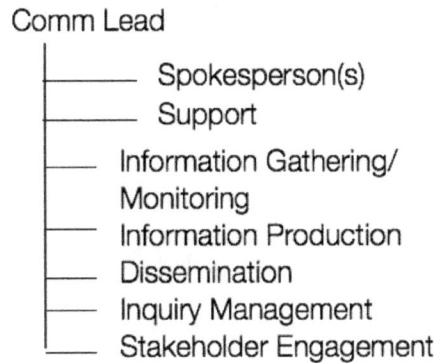

Comm Lead
———— Spokesperson(s)
———— Support
———— Information Gathering/
            Monitoring
———— Information Production
———— Dissemination
———— Inquiry Management
———— Stakeholder Engagement

Let me stop here for just a minute and explain why I have chosen to organize a team in this particular way. The truth is there are all kinds of ways of organizing a team. What often happens in a response, particularly in an organization without a thought-through plan, is that they try to get their work done pretty much the same way they do every day. It is natural in an event when things and people are flying around, to stay close to the tried and true, to stick to the familiar. But there are a few good reasons why this particular organization chart is effective, so before you throw it out and go to the tried and true, you may want to consider these reasons:

1) It is intuitive as it follows the communications process.
2) It follows closely the National Response Team Joint Information Center Model.

> If you are in an event where you need to collaborate with police, fire, emergency management or any state, local or federal government agency, they will likely use this same approach. This means you'll be playing the same game with the same rules.

It is the most standard communication process used as part of the National Incident Management System

3) It makes it easier to incorporate new players on your team

Because this basic model is a widely adopted standard, new people can fit in easily, particularly if they have any JIC training or experience

4) It is highly scalable.

This structure works for the smallest events as well as the largest.

5) It works.

This basic structure has been used effectively in numerous events, both large and small. And where others structures have failed for a variety of reasons, this organization structure is widely seen as the most effective.

Scalability

In almost any event almost every job is important and must be done. An exception may be in Engagement—not every event may require a person or a team to work directly and personally with people and groups with high interest in the event. But, some events are small and some are very large. In small events, two or three people do the work of everyone. In very large events, each of these operational groups expands with additional team members assigned.

Small event structure

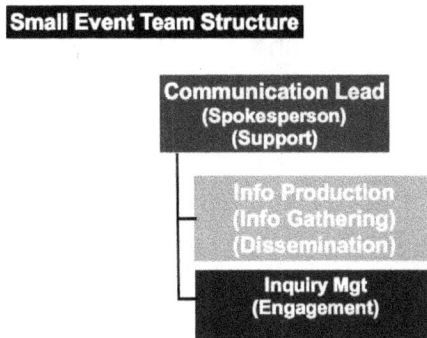

Small Event Team Structure

Communication Lead
(Spokesperson)
(Support)

Info Production
(Info Gathering)
(Dissemination)

Inquiry Mgt
(Engagement)

In this structure, the Communication Lead, Spokesperson and Support roles are combined into one. Information Gathering, which includes Monitoring, is combined with Information Production and Dissemination. And the person assigned to Inquiry Management also handles any engagement requirements.

There is no one magic way of doing this. Depending on the communication technology used, it may make more sense to have the person managing inquiries to also handle dissemination. The primary point is to have a clearly defined structure with clearly defined responsibilities.

Large event structure

In a large event, the overall structure remains the same, but additional team members are added to each of the operational units. The operational units are divided into sub-units or groups. This is very important that the basic functional units remain the same because it simplifies training, and provides a manageable span of control for the Communication Lead. In very large events, leaders for each of the sub-units will also be identified. Maintaining span of control is important and is one of the essential elements of the

National Incident Management System and the Incident Command System. Ideally five people would be the maximum direct reports for any leader, but no more than seven. By sub-dividing the main functional units into smaller sub-units maintains the span of control for each of the functional units.

Do not be daunted by this larger structure. Even if you do not face events of sufficient scope and duration to need a very large team, it is helpful to review each of the sub-units to understand some of the details you will run into. Having a good picture of this larger structure in mind, or having it readily available during an event, will help you or whoever is the Communication Lead to effectively delegate the details.

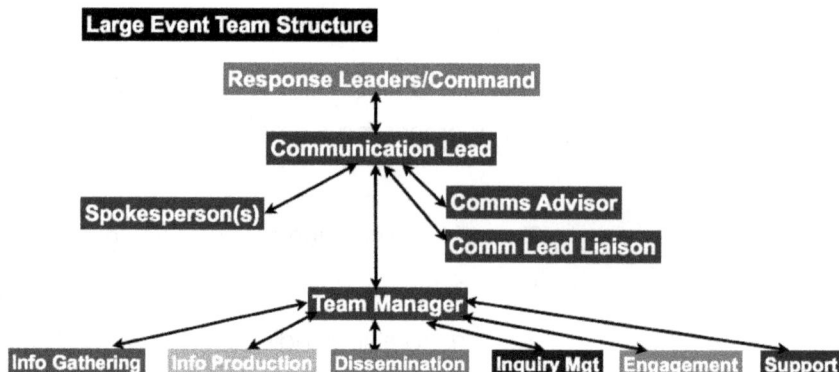

Large Event Team Structure

Response Leaders/Command

Communication Lead

Spokesperson(s)   Comms Advisor

Comm Lead Liaison

Team Manager

Info Gathering | Info Production | Dissemination | Inquiry Mgt | Engagement | Support

This chart shows the complete team. But in a large response team members may be located in various locations. And there likely will be many people assigned to some of the sub-units. For example, a natural disaster may be spread over a large area and you may need to have team members dispersed or even create different but linked teams in various locations. In events with lots of media coverage, particularly over an extended period of time, you will likely need many people assigned to the Media Inquiry unit. And for events such as environmental disasters caused by a toxic release or oil spill where many people and communities are affected, you will likely need a large number of team members assigned to the Government and Community Relations units.

To give some idea of the relative sizes of the units in major events, the following chart can be used to help identify the resources you may need to call on for the highest level crises or emergencies.

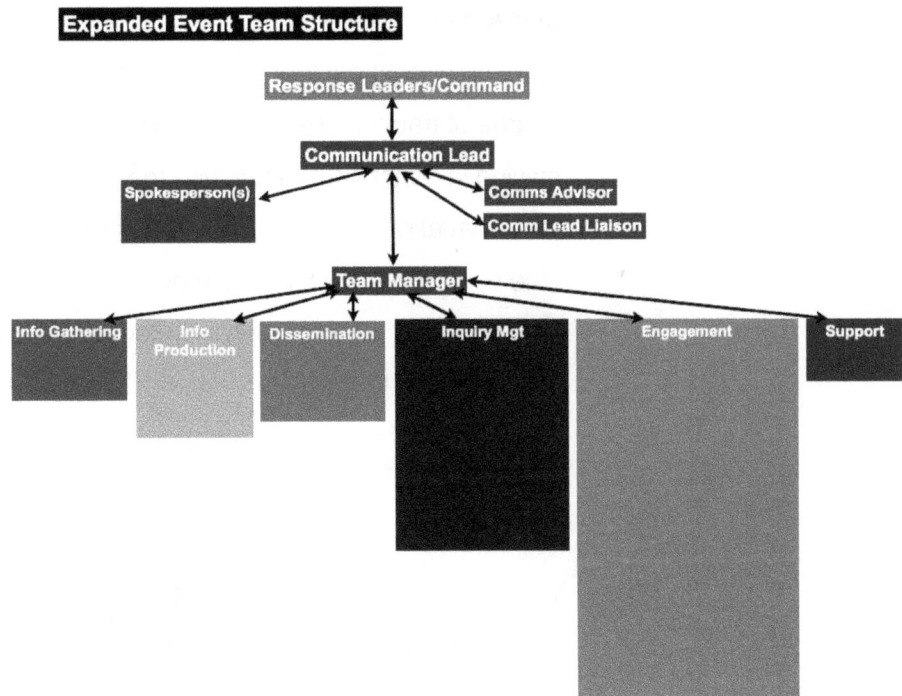

Expanded Event Team Structure

Response Leaders/Command

Communication Lead

Spokesperson(s)

Comms Advisor

Comm Lead Liaison

Team Manager

Info Gathering

Info Production

Dissemination

Inquiry Mgt

Engagement

Support

A Smoothly Running Machine

If you haven't had a lot of experience in crisis communications in large organizations and for some good-sized events, it may be hard to picture how this all works. Since I'm using the machine analogy, any confusion you may experience may be like me looking at all the parts of an engine resting on a workbench. My thought is: how in the world do all these go together so that they actually burn gasoline and move a vehicle?

So, let's try and get a picture in our heads of what this structure looks like when it is operating properly and running like a well-tuned engine.

You are the Communication Lead and you got through the initial startup phase. At least some of your team has assembled, both in a pre-set location and some have joined online using your advanced communication management platform. The crisis is unfolding rapidly with new twists and turns on almost a minute-by-minute basis. But now you have a person in charge of tracking that information and she has some help. So they are staying in constant contact with the people directly involved in responding to the situation as well as monitoring the media and social media in real-time using the sophisticated monitoring tools your organization has invested in—as well as the free ones like Google Alerts, Twitscoop and others.

Managing the calls

The volume of questions from phone calls and emails has been rising—it started off with a bang almost the same time you were notified of the crisis. You dealt with them quickly by referring to the Initial Statement on the website as soon as you got that launched and published. Plus, you put out a tweet and a Facebook post linking back to your now live incident website. But already that initial statement is in need of updating. Your Information Production team is busy processing the continual feeds of raw info coming from the Information Gathering team and very quickly you get your first request for approval to release. It's a simple update of information. You have a question about one item, and refer to the person leading the response—for convenience sake, we'll call that person the Incident Commander. He says it is good to go and you quickly get back to your

Team Manager and say, publish. It immediately goes out through the incident website, through your Facebook, Twitter, Google+ and whatever other channels you have set up. Plus, you direct the Team Manager now to email the updates both to the expanded media list you've pre-built in your communication management system and to the rapidly growing list of visitors who come to your site requesting to be added to your update list. Some request text updates and some emails.

The Team Manager checks in with the Dissemination team making sure they are publishing the approved update on the incident site and fully linked to the social media channels you are using. With your communication management system, the team involved in answering questions—the Inquiry team—is using the latest approved update to answer the questions coming in. All inquiries are tracked in the web-based system; some automatically when coming in using the form on the incident website, some automatically through emails designated for that purposed and linked to your communication management system. The phone calls are all logged. The Team Manager uses her laptop to check on the inquiries coming in and notes a question asked by three reporters about an issue involving the organization and the response. The Team Manager brings it to your attention, you confirm that the question reflects a rumor and you direct the Team Manager to include the correct information in the next update to dispel the rumor.

You let the Team Manager know that a briefing with the response team leaders, of which you are the one designated to deal with response information and reputation issues, will begin in ten minutes and likely last an hour. You tell the Team Manager that she has authority to approve minor updates of already established information, but major new issues should be brought to your attention. A "runner" is identified to run to the conference room where your briefing is to be held and alert you of any emerging issues or need for approvals. Other issues coming up in the team can be handled by text messages which you can read during the briefing.

You check with the Team Manager to make certain that all the logistics needs of the communication team are met and you are assured that the Support Manager has been doing a great job of going to all the unit leads and checking in with their staffing, equipment, supplies, IT requirements. The Team Manager also reports that a press conference is assumed and that preparations are being made to set up the designated facility and prepare the talking points and graphics needed for the response leaders for the conference.

Managing approvals

The two of you are interrupted briefly to look over another update prepared by Information Production. You look at your watch. Six minutes since the last one. That's good. You approve this for release knowing that it fits in the parameters that you had worked out with organization management and the Incident Commander in advance allowing you to approve certain information while preserving their right to approve more significant messages. You set some guidelines for the Team Manager: updates every 15 minutes, even if info changes are minimal, and inquiry response time of no less than 20 minutes. You also tell her to prepare for a press conference in two hours which you will recommend to the response leadership, and to request that the Support Manager place the Red Engagement teams on standby. You'll discuss with response leadership the need to begin engaging government officials and community members.

Monitoring

Just prior to leaving for the briefing, you ask to talk to the Information Gathering manager. "What's happening with the media and social media?" you ask. Twitter activity has been rising steadily and shows no sign of letting up, but some potentially significant issues are emerging. He tells you that he has alerted Information Production to those issues and is working with the response organization to confirm or clarify those issues. The crisis is generating quite a few videos from those outside the organization but so far none have caused a major issue. One is being investigated as potentially coming from an unrelated previous event. Several family members of employees have been commenting on Facebook, in some cases with some rather disparaging comments about the organization, and you ask the Team Manager to involve HR in working with Information Production and Dissemination to make certain employees and family members are getting the best possible information, as well as reminding them of your organization's social media policies. Media reports have mostly used the updates you have provided but have added some video and interviews with people impacted by the event. A storyline is emerging relating to who will be held accountable for this and you think this issue through on your way to the briefing.

The machine is running. No, not everything is smooth. The Team Manager told you about the little tussle going on between the Multi-Media Specialist and the Information Production Lead over graphic styles. You've got some big issues to discuss with leadership about the "blame game" that is emerging in some media reports. You know that a lot of media focus is going to be on the emotional human impacts of this event and you want to advise leadership on how best to deal with this that shows above all the concern that your organization has for those affected. You know you will have to deal with some potential push-back from legal on some of the messages you want conveyed. You know that at least one powerful person on the response leadership team is going to object to your plans for elected official engagement. But good information is being gathered from multiple sources, it's being produced in appropriate forms, the approval process— while still too slow—seems to be largely working to protect against major errors, inquiries are being handled and the team is gaining efficiency. There are good comments on social media channels about all the communication channels being employed and timeliness of updates. You have a good picture of sentiment and emerging trends and you are prepared to give a report on what's happening in communication to the response team leadership. You enter the room, not satisfied, but still reasonably confident. The machine is running.

Sure, this is an overly simplified picture. The "fog of war" certainly applies to any major event I have been involved in. But the purpose of this illustration is not to precisely describe what happens in any particular situation as much as make clear why the "machine" is so important. One of the most common and significant problems I have seen in many events is that a very talented communication manager tries to do in a big event what they do every day. They try to do too many jobs, control too many things, be in too many places at once. It fails. The solution lies in having the appropriate technology that supports maximum efficiency, but also having a great team of people who know exactly what they are supposed to do. When you do, the machine can be a beautiful thing.

Primary Roles Overview

We're starting with a quick overview of the primary roles, then will go into more details in the Plan Operational Details below. We're saving the complete job descriptions for each of the roles in this plan for the appendix including a graphic illustration of how the people filling these roles interact with each in doing their jobs.

Communication Lead—two jobs: 1) Advise the leaders running the response about the public communication requirements, reputation implications and impact of their actions and words on trust, and 2) lead the entire team to achieve the communication objectives

Team Manager—Lead the team, free the Communication Lead so he/she can do their job in advising the leaders, carry out the strategies and plans of the Communication Lead

Information Gathering Manager—Collect all the information you can about the event from internal and external sources and provide that for processing into information and messages to be distributed. Also provide Communication Lead with continuing situation awareness.

Information Production Manager—Produce all the information and products needed by various audiences in a way that meets the communication objectives, that meets the information demands and is suitable for the multiple communication channels being used

Dissemination Manager—Select, prepare and use the communication channels appropriate for the different audiences to insure distribution of the information and messages and that maximizes opportunity for direct engagement

Inquiry Manager—Make certain that questions asked of the team are answered correctly, appropriately and quickly. Use the information gained from the questions and engagements with audiences to help the Communication Lead inform response leaders and provide appropriate guidance on actions and priorities.

Engagement Manager—Plan for and manage direct interactions with audiences particularly government officials, community leaders and members and response partners

Support Manager—Continually assess needs of the team and insure that they have what they need to do their jobs

In smaller events, the people assigned to the primary roles may be able to manage the event. You may even be able to combine some of those roles in one person as illustrated in the small scale event graphic. But now we're going to talk about how to scale up to a big, or a really big event.

The good thing about this plan is that the basic structure doesn't change from the smallest event to the largest. But larger events require many more people and that means you have to know where they need to be assigned in order for the whole machine to continue to work well. As you add people, the responsibilities of one of the primary roles are broken up into individual assignments. For example, instead of one writer working in Information Production, you may need several writers and may assign one for the standard updates, another for background information and fact sheets, and another to prepare talking point and work with the spokespersons.

Major Roles

In the Appendix you will find detailed job descriptions for each of the roles included in this plan. Here we will focus on each of the areas of the workflow, how they are sub-categorized and also how they relate to and work with each other. We will also briefly state where appropriate the corresponding role in the Joint Information Center Model.

Communication Lead

Spokespersons

Communication Advisor

Communication Lead Liaison

Team Manager

Information Gathering

Information Production

Dissemination

Inquiry Management

Stakeholder Engagement

Support

Leadership Interaction

Communication Lead

This person, the equivalent of the Public Information Officer or PIO in the JIC Model, is the leader of the entire communication effort. He or she is responsible for all aspects of the communication activities including advising the leaders responding to the event on any and all actions and messages that bear on the public's understanding of the event and response and the reputation of the organization or organizations involved. It is easy to see how important it is that this person be a seasoned and skillful communications professional. Key capabilities include being calm under pressure, being able to effectively delegate and hold people accountable, having a strategic mind and keeping a strategic perspective, and being able to command the respect and attention of high-performing leaders who themselves are under great stress and pressure.

There are two essential but often competing demands on this person. First, to be a central and highly engaged member of the leadership group (called Command or Unified Command in the Incident Command System). And second, to lead the communication team and operations. In the early stages of most incidents as the communication team is being activated, assembled and organized, the Communication Lead must provide many of the essential functions. But as the team begins to coalesce it is very important that the Communication Lead delegate responsibility and move more deeply into the advisory role on the leadership team. While doing this, it is also essential that the Communication Lead continue to track and monitor all activities and step in when it is necessary to readjust the team, strategies or activities.

The Team Manager's ability to manage the communication operation will largely determine how free the Communication Lead is to perform their advisory and guidance functions. There must be a high level of trust and confidence between these two people for the communication machine to run smoothly.

In this plan the Spokespersons fall under the management of the Communication Lead. This may be controversial as in major events the most senior person or persons in the organization may very well serve as the primary spokespersons and these people don't typically report to a mere communication manager. However, either the Communication Lead is held responsible for the communications or is not. And how the spokespeople perform and maintain message discipline has some of the greatest impacts on the success of the communication effort. This would be a valuable part of the plan to discuss with senior leaders prior to an actual event in order to avoid confusion and miscommunication.

The Communication Lead must work closely with the spokespersons to help make certain they are getting the latest and best information to provide, that they are and remain effective in media opportunities, that they maintain information and message discipline (sticking to facts and the key messages and not wandering into dangerous waters), and that they keep an appropriate level of visibility related to media and public expectations. If it is clear that the spokesperson, even if it the CEO or Chairman, has lost credibility and is no longer a positive contributor to building trust and a positive reputation, it is necessary that the Communication Lead have the ability to deal decisively with this situation. Failure to reign in or effectively manage a CEO or senior leader serving as spokesperson is the sad story of too many reputation crises.

Spokesperson(s)   The spokespersons are the visible presence of the organization and the response team. This role is diminishing in significance to some degree as the role of media overall is diminishing in how information is conveyed and public perceptions formed. Nevertheless, an effective spokesperson still is one of the most significant elements of a successful crisis communication response and conversely, many excellent efforts at communication were completely discounted by the failures of a spokesperson or spokespersons.

An effective spokesperson has these important qualities:

- is deeply knowledgeable about the organization, the event and the response

- understands that how messages are communicated in this visual era is often more important than what is communicated

- has the ability to create connections with audiences even through the medium of TV or video

- genuinely feels empathy for those impacted and can effectively and sincerely communicate that empathy, verbally and non-verbally

- communicates humility and is willing to admit that they don't know everything

- shows strength and resolve in the face of often extreme stress and inordinate difficulties

- understands that honesty and transparency are keys to building credibility

Yes, that is asking a lot and the list could go on quite awhile. The strange thing about the spokesperson is that the public's perception of the organization is very much tied up to the public's personal and emotional response to the person as mediated through the Internet or TV screen. That's why a CEO or senior leader who is exceptionally capable in many respects but cannot effectively represent the organization because of personal characteristics that show up when interviewed should not serve as spokesperson or serve a very, very limited role publicly.

Lessons for spokespersons

This manual isn't about media training or spokesperson training so we can't go into important details here. But the sad record of many recent events teaches a few key lessons:

You may lose the spokesperson

Given today's media environment, an organization that does significant harm to people, property or the environment will likely pay a high price, and that price will often fall on the most visible spokesperson. That is why there is wisdom in carefully considering who will take that visible role understanding that the person may be lost to the organization as a result of being the spokesperson.

24/7 visibility vs. over-exposure

The balance between visibility and over-exposure is very fine. A CEO, Chairman or senior leaders must be visible in an event that brings the organization to full public attention. But that visibility must be balanced by controlled exposure. Fatigue and the sheer omnipresence of reporters and even members of the public who will broadcast what is said and heard means it is only a matter of time that a serious gaffe will occur. When I say gaffe, I don't even mean that the person says something bad or irresponsible, but that by clipping it and taking it out of context it can be used to portray the spokesperson and therefore the organization negatively. This unfortunate reality is best prevented by limiting visibility and continually reminding spokespersons of the importance of message discipline.

Sticking to the message

Maintaining message and information discipline can be very hard as there is a natural tendency to want to openly and sincerely answer questions posed by reporters. But there is a good reason why the information management processes described in this plan are implemented. Information discipline means that only authorized, approved and verified information is released. This insures that whatever comes from the organization is correct which is important to maintaining credibility. Message discipline means not being tempted to wander off into topics that are not essential or even dangerous. It means sticking to the key messages that have been carefully developed even if it means they are being repeated over and over. It also means getting over the feeling that every question must be answered. The skill of delivering the key messages despite a barrage of tempting questions is one that is essential in the training of any potential spokesperson.

Communication Advisor

The Communication Advisor does not typically appear in many communication plans, including most that I have written over the years. It is an optional role, but one I believe can be very important. The Communication Advisor should be a senior crisis communication professional who has deep experience in major crisis events and who also is very knowledgeable about the organization and the types of crises that can occur. Their job is simple in concept: keep a 30,000 foot view of the entire situation and be attached to the Communication Lead to help provide, advice, perspective and judgment. I believe it is almost essential that this person be outside of the organization and not an employee. That means he or she will have the freedom to be honest and give straightforward advice. A consultant has more freedom to express dangerous opinions for the good of the organization because, while they may lose a client if the danger proves real, they do not typically lose their jobs. For example, it may become clear to the Communication Advisor that the highly regarded CEO of an organization who is serving as spokesperson for the event has irreparably lost his or her credibility and to continue in that role will cause significant damage to the organization. A Communication Lead who serves under the CEO in normal times may find it difficult or impossible to advocate for the CEO's removal as spokesperson. But a Communication Advisor, particularly one that is committed to serving the best interests of the organization rather than his or her own self-interests, may be in a much better position to advise the response leaders and perhaps the board (or elected officials overseeing an agency) that the removal of the CEO is essential.

One challenge you may face is finding a Communication Advisor who is both a seasoned, experienced professional with proven judgment and who has an in-depth understanding of the realities of today's hyper-connected, Internet-dominated, social media world. Since qualities are essential, it may be advisable to incorporate into the communication leadership two outside professionals who combined provide the perspective that is needed.

The Communication Advisor typically will participate with the Communication Lead in many if not all of the meetings and briefings of the response leadership team. It may be necessary for confidentiality to allow only company employees or those under specific Non-Disclosure Agreements to participate in some meetings and in those situations, the Communication Lead must bring the Communication Advisor into the picture as much as is possible given the constraints.

The Communication Advisor must also be given free reign to view and evaluate the communication team and its operation. One key role that Communication Advisor must be able to play is to help evaluate the team and the performance of individual team members, advising the Communication Lead on recommended changes. Being outside of the organization again helps in providing more perspective and freedom to evaluate and recommend difficult decisions.

Communication Lead Liaison

The communication team and the response leadership group (or JIC and Unified Command in ICS parlance) are typically separated to some degree. They may be separated by a door and a wall if in the same building, or they could be across the street, on another floor or even a further distance away. While proximity is valuable, so is separation. But this separation means that it can be very difficult for the Communication Lead to effectively fill both key roles: advisor to response leaders and manager of the communication team. There are two roles that can help the Communication Lead perform effectively without losing their mind. One is the Team Manager (or JIC Manager) and the other is the Communication Lead Liaison.

This role is not typically found in organization charts including the JIC Model, but I have found myself in this role and have implemented it in major drills and events very effectively when I served as Communication Lead. It might be more accurate to call this person a "runner." Because what they often need to do is go back and forth between the meeting place of the response leaders when the Communication Lead is in the meetings and the communication team's location. Certainly, messages can be conveyed by cell phone, text, radios, landlines, email and the like. But sometimes there is no substitute for someone who can carry documents for review and signing, who can relay urgency and interrupt the participation of the Communication Lead in the meeting if the situation warrants.

[A comment about the term Liaison. Using Liaison as a reference to a role like this one is very appropriate given the specific function they play. But, a plan that aims to be fully compliant with the National Incident Management System (NIMS) and the Incident Command System (ICS) should probably avoid using the term "liaison" for any role except the specific "Liaison Officer" role as identified in ICS. This is to avoid confusion. The Liaison Officer in ICS is a member of the Command Staff focused specifically on coordinating information and activities with response organizations that are actively engaged in the response but not a member of Unified Command.]

Communication Team Manager

The Crisis Communication Team Manager or Team Manager, as we'll refer to them here, is one of the most critical roles in the communication response. An effective manager will relieve the Communication Lead from many of the operational details of the team, allowing them to focus on advising the response leaders and setting overall direction for the communications.

The equivalent role in the Joint Information Center model is the JIC Manager.

The Communication Lead must be available to the response team and actively participate in response decisions, must keep a clear head and perspective, must remain strategic, and must be free to focus on the most significant and urgent issues. All of these are dependent on a competent Team Manager who will take charge of the communication team and implement the plans and strategies laid out by the Communication Lead.

What does a good Team Manager look like?

Here are a few qualities and skills important to being successful in this role:

- The Team Manager needs to have the full trust and confidence of the Communication Lead.

- He or she should be able to step in and fill the role of Communication Lead for protracted events or in a situation

64

where the Communication Lead is no longer able to fill that role. The Team Manager is in reality the Deputy Communication Lead.

- The Team Manager typically assigns team members to their roles and in that they must either know in advance or quickly evaluate the skills, qualities and experience of activated team members and organize them to maximize their contributions.

- Continual performance monitoring and assessment of the effectiveness of each team member is a key part of the job, and the Team Manager must be decisive in making changes if they become necessary.

- The Team Manager is also a coach, guiding and encouraging team members, teaching the specific requirements of each role if they are not adequately trained and motivating them to maximum effectiveness.

- While the focus of the Team Manager is tactics and details, they must also think strategically. The "fog of war" is common in large-scale events, but the Team Manager must sort out through all the requirements to help the team stay focused on meeting key objectives.

- The Team Manager is the primary conduit to the Communication Lead on all the response communication activities and so must be able to prioritize issues, requirements and provide very brief but complete reporting on all activities. The ability of the Communication Lead to properly advise the response leaders depends on this reporting and the guidance provided by the Team Manager.

Information Gathering

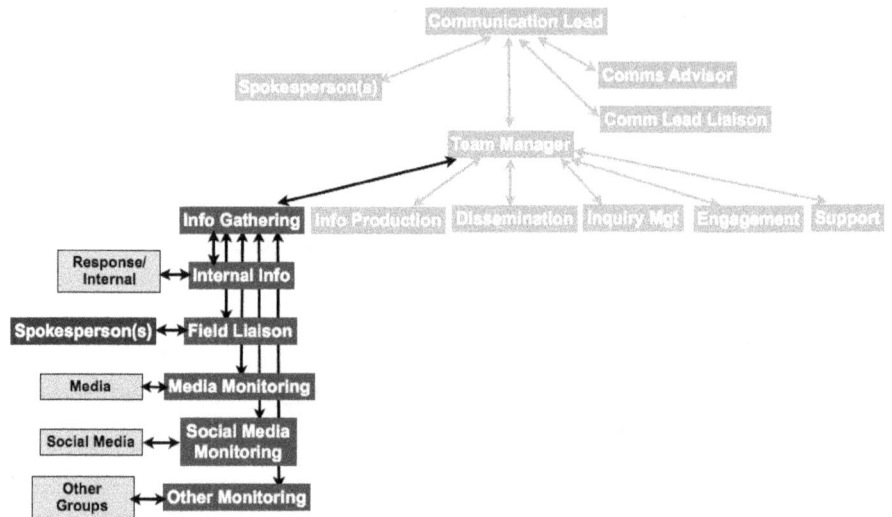

Information Gathering Lead

All the best efforts of the entire team will be for nothing if the team does not have access to the best information about the event, the response activities, and the external factors such as government response, media coverage and public conversation. Too often plans emphasize the role of the communication team as the "voice" of the response and the organization responding without giving proper focus on the "ears" of the response which is the Information Gathering function. I like to remind communicators that God gave us two ears and one mouth and we should take the hint. Because building trust is the overarching objective of the communication activity, the Information Gathering Lead must clearly see their task as uncovering all the vital information needed to build trust.

The process of gathering information has become more complex and challenging in the past few years. Prior to the Internet and its impact on events, the communication team gathered information exclusively from the response organization itself. Media monitoring was also done but that was accomplished by using broadcast monitoring services and press clipping services, or even by bringing TV monitors into the communication operation.

Now information gathering includes gathering the best possible information from sources both internal to the response and external sources.

Gathering information from internal sources

Internal sources are those directly under the control of the response leaders. In an Incident Command System event, it is relatively easy to identify the people and positions with whom the Information Gathering unit needs to connect. The Planning Section is responsible for gathering all response-related information and in larger events a special sub-unit of this section, the Situation Status unit, is specifically tasked with gathering and making available event information available to response leaders. In ICS responses, an individual would be positioned with the Situation Status unit to provide a continuous feed of information about the event and response activities to the communication team.

If your organization does not use ICS, then it is necessary to determine how the organization gathers, assimilates, analyzes and presents event and response information to the response leaders. This should be done prior to an event occurring or even a drill so that the Communication Lead and Information Gathering Lead have a clear idea of how to gather the best information and any issues relating to this gathering of information can be dealt with prior to an event.

In larger events, it will be necessary to assign several communication team members to the Information Gathering unit. Severe weather or other events spread out over a geographic area will likely require several communication team members, as will events involving different facilities or locations. The risk analysis process is necessary to understand how many team members will be needed for what types and scope of events.

Field Liaison

Larger events and geographically dispersed events will likely require several spokespersons who may be assigned to different sites or event locations. The expanded plan calls for a position in the Information Gathering Unit called Field Liaison. This is a communication team member assigned to assist the spokesperson by making certain they have access to the latest approved information and the key messages. However, the reason that this position falls under Information Gathering rather than Dissemination in this plan is because an important responsibility of that role is to gather information from the field. Media monitoring is done by this person by understanding the questions that are being asked of the spokesperson as well as probing the reporters for information they may have. Being in the field also gives the Field Liaison the opportunity to observe activities, gather sentiment information from stakeholders and the public and to interact with responders in the field who may be closest to the operational response.

Obstacles to internal info gathering

Obstacles Specific to Internal Information Gathering

There are many obstacles the Information Gathering Lead or team must overcome to do a thorough job of collecting information. The job requires the nose for news and tenacity of a hardened journalist. But one obstacle that often arises can and should be addressed prior to any event. This is the reluctance of many involved in the response to share what they know with the communication team for fear of that information being released to the media or public. This is an understandable fear. However, if those who have vital information are unwilling to provide it to the communication team, this mistrust will translate into much slower and less accurate delivery of response information. In an ICS response, the way to deal with this is simple: Ask the person withholding information if they are the Incident Commander. If not, by withholding information they are assuming the prerogative that belongs only to the Incident Commander who has the sole authority to determine what information can be released to the public or withheld. This issue is so important it needs to be embodied in the crisis or emergency response plan of the organization. Even if the plan does not follow the ICS model it should state specifically that only the leader with authority over the response can authorize release or withhold release of public information and all responders should provide what they know as soon as possible to the communication team.

Monitoring

Gathering information from external sources

Today the most important information about an event often comes from external rather than internal sources. There is no area of crisis response that demonstrates how much our world has changed than this. In the past, the responders had access to virtually all the important information. There was time to gather it, process it, approve it and provide it to the media for distribution to the public. Now, in all but the most invisible events, the information about the event and what is happening is shared by anyone who has any information about it at all. Often, it doesn't even require that. Opinions and perspectives are shared without any access to real information.

This "crowd sourcing" of information about events is dramatically changing the role of the communication team involved with the response. Where before the goal of crisis communicators was to be "the first and best source" of information about the event, now it is impossible in all but the most closed events to be the first. But, that leaves being the best source of information which is dependent on knowing the information that is being distributed and quickly confirming or correcting the false information that is a very common result of the crowd sourcing and speed of distribution through the Internet. In other words: Rumor Management. This process, once a small part of a standard communication plan, has taken front and center because of the role of the Internet and social networking. That means that monitoring is now one of the most critical and essential elements of the operation.

Monitoring refers to gathering information about the event, event activities and sentiments about the response from non-response sources.

Media monitoring

Media monitoring has been a traditional element of most crisis communication plans. This was done through clipping services, through broadcast monitoring services and even using TV monitors in the emergency center. Most media monitoring can now be done using the Internet. Standard searches and tools such as Google Alerts can identify stories almost as soon as they emerge. These are supplemented by a large number of media monitoring systems that can provide copyrighted clips of print stories, website news site stories, blogs, video postings, and cable TV. Many organizations use these tools on a daily basis which simply means that the staff involved in daily monitoring need to be incorporated into the Information Gathering unit.

Social media monitoring

The line between social media monitoring and media monitoring is not at all clear. For one thing, the definition of media is changing. The best definition of media I've heard is from my colleague Marc Mullen who defines it as "anyone who amplifies the message." Given that many using social media have very large networks, that in turn are connected to others with very large networks, the media in this definition can include a single person who retweets or sends an email. Because the news from official news sources has largely moved onto the Internet it shares the same space with all the "unofficial news" that constitutes the information and comments from the crowd about the event. This means that the Internet and its search tools are used for media monitoring but also used for social media monitoring.

In addition to the search engines and alert systems available, social media monitoring can be done using many free tools such as Twitter, Twitscoop,

Hootsuite and many others. There are many excellent guides available but since the social media world involves very rapid change, these tools should be evaluated continually. In addition to the free tools, a large number of monitoring systems are available as a subscription service. Many organizations are continually monitoring social media which means in a crisis this activity needs to be ramped up and additional team members assigned.

Other monitoring

Events may require additional monitoring in order to gain an accurate, actionable understanding of the event and reaction to it. For example, certain groups or communities may be deeply impacted by an event in which case it would be advisable to monitor the reactions of this group. Certain individual stakeholders or groups may also be critical to monitor and general sentiment monitoring through the Internet would not likely be sufficient. Monitoring may be done in these ways:

Listening posts—these are trusted people who are either already involved in the group or who can become involved in order to gain an understanding of the group's reactions and sentiments

Online surveys or forms—interactive surveys or forms can be created and sent to or made available to members of the group to gather reactions, questions, comments and sentiment

Surveys—either scientifically validated surveys or snapshot surveys can be conducted to gain a more complete picture

Direct observation—in some cases it is necessary or highly advisable for the response leaders, the Communication Lead or the Information Gathering Lead to visit the affected areas, meet with individuals and groups and personally monitor the reactions.

This monitoring, particularly if it involves the community or government, is typically done in close coordination with the Engagement unit.

Information Sharing

The information gathered by this unit must get to the appropriate people on the crisis communication team with the minimum delay. The primary initial users of the information are the Information Production unit and the communication leaders. The Communication Lead and the Team Manager must have access on a continuing basis to all the information coming in so they can make decisions about priorities, about changes in strategy and direction and so they can provide response leaders with information the leaders need to make decisions. The Information Production unit needs the raw information as quickly as possible so they can begin the process of preparing it for approval and release.

The best practice for sharing this information is to use a web-based or cloud platform that is designed specifically for gathering, sharing and processing information for release. While there are a very limited number of special-purpose applications for this, such as PIER (full disclosure statement), broader purpose applications and tools such as Google Docs, OfficeLive, Sharepoint, Basecamp and many other tools can be prepared for efficient use in information sharing. Web-based storage systems like Dropbox can also be used to facilitate the development and editing of materials. While many still use organization email and organization-specific networks, this can create significant challenges when in a major event contractors, lawyers, subject matter experts and others are needed to actively participate. It becomes even more of an issue in a joint response with government agencies including first response agencies. If these systems are used, they need to allow access to all team participants.

Initial Information Analysis

It should not be considered the job of the Information Gathering Team to analyze and prioritize the raw information. Nor should it be their job to verify the facts. To do so may take focus off from gathering the raw information. However, if the event is very fast moving with many different team members supplying information, it will be necessary for the Information Gathering Lead to include a very initial analysis in their responsibility. This may simply be re-ordering of the documents or bullet items with the information, or it may be creating special alerts via text, cell phone or email, to the Information Production Lead, Team Manager and Communication Lead for items seen to be as particularly significant.

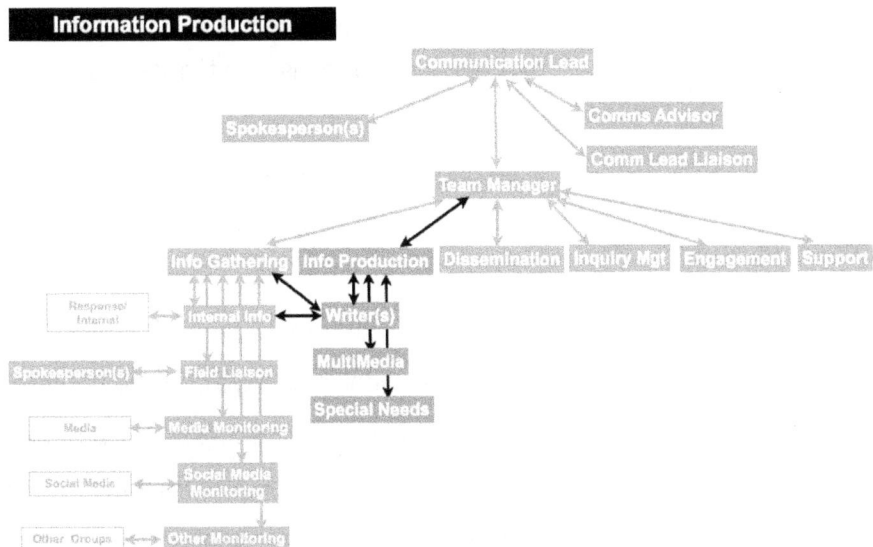

Information Production

Information Production Lead

The Information Production Lead's job is to prepare the raw information into approved, releasable and useful formats. This includes all information from the standard information updates and fact sheets to visuals, maps, charts, videos, presentation materials, printed flyers and more.

**Info Production
now vs. then**

The formats and styles of information needed to communicate about a crisis or emergency have changed along with the communication channels. In the recent past, the press release was the primary format for information. It included the key facts about the event in classic inverted pyramid order and quotations from appropriate spokespersons. Today, the press release has largely been replaced by tweets on Twitter, Facebook posts, and information updates emailed to audiences and published on a website or websites. Images and video have become important elements of almost all communication today including crisis communication. Text alerts, automated phone messages are also important means of communicating. RSS feeds and widgets are frequently used to help distribute messages via other websites. More about the various channels to be used will be covered under Dissemination, but here we need to focus on the types of information needed and the styles and formats used.

If we understand how audiences get information now compared to how they used to get it, we can better understand the style and format changes required. In the Walter Cronkite or even Dan Rather era, most news was scheduled, highly processed and linear. We could read the paper in the morning or evening and we could watch the evening news at 6 p.m. and 11 p.m. News was highly processed which means that professional journalists and editors created the story from the raw material, deciding which facts and elements were important and in what order. And it was linear in that the full control of what the audience received was in the hands of the sender: first this, then this, then after the commercial break, you will get this. Now news and public information is unscheduled, largely unprocessed and non-linear. That means it is available all the time and in all places; it is most often very raw and unprocessed; and when, how and in what order it is accessed is determined by the audience not the sender.

This dramatic change means that crisis communication now is a continuous process of updating audiences, not a scheduled one. It means that the speed of information is so fast that there is little time or need for the kind of processing or careful crafting and presenting that was needed before. In fact, audiences react against this kind of careful crafting as lacking transparency and authenticity. The information must also be made available for audiences to access how and when they want. That means multiple channels, it also means different levels of detail and depth available to audiences allowing them to control the information they get.

The difference between "information" and "messages."

Information and Messages

The terms "information" and "messages" are often interchangeable, yet there are some important differences. Communication professionals and senior leaders may have very different ideas about the priority to be communicated in an incident: is it more important to communicate the information about the event, or is it more important to convey the important messages the organization wants received? As an example, emergency management professionals are typically much more focused on communicating the facts about an event and the response (information). But the political leaders they work for are most often far more focused on communicating key messages intended to demonstrate the concern and commitment of the leaders.

Both are very important. But, they are not the same and it is helpful for the Information Production Lead to have a clear understanding of the differences. Information is focused on facts, statements that can be determined to be true or false, such as: "We have confirmed that three people have been seriously injured are in the hospital." A message example is typically not factual in the sense of being provable: "We are concerned about the public's health and safety above all." Messages are more human, convey emotion and communicate intention.

While differences in priorities and strategies will emerge and there are no firmly established rules, the following guidelines are presented to help the communication team achieve the primary goal of crisis and emergency communication which is building and maintaining trust:

Actions speak louder than words.

The ability of an organization to emerge successfully through a crisis is based to the greatest degree on the audience's perception of the character of those in charge. Much research has established that fact. But character is judged more by action than by words. That means that what an organization does in response to a crisis is more important than what it says. Clear, simple straightforward communication about the facts of the actions taken fall under the information category, but are the most important in conveying the message that the organization cares about those affected.

Messages connect people.

Effective messages enable your audience to connect to the people involved in the response. Audiences want to see that the people responsible for managing an event are people they can relate to, they can respect and trust.

Messages are most powerfully conveyed visually.

Understanding that audiences are looking to place trust and confidence in the leaders places a high importance on how the message is delivered visually. Non-verbal cues that are inconsistent with high words of empathy and care are devastating. Spokespersons need to be trained, tested and proven that they can connect with audiences and communicate real concern and care through their visual presentation before being thrust into the forefront of a crisis.

Empathy and concern are the most important message.

Dr. Vincent Covello teaches: they won't care what you know until they know that you care. Care is the single most important message. It needs to be conveyed in words (good), in the manner in which the message is communicated (better) but primarily in strong action that puts meaning into the words (best). A CEO or response leader cannot stand before the audience and say "We care" when the actions taken by the organization do not clearly demonstrate that.

Information becomes most important once trust and respect are established.

When a crisis or emergency communication devolves into nothing more than talking points for political leaders, as happens frequently in high-profile events, a fundamental fact is forgotten. People want to know what is going on, what progress s being made, what prevention measures are being implemented, updates on investigations into causes and all the relevant facts of a response. While political leaders and reputation-sensitive organization leaders may want to keep focused on messages, it should never be forgotten that the primary task of crisis communicators is to communicate the essential facts about an event and what is being done about it.

Documents Chart   *Common Formats and Document Types*

Channel	Description	Importance	Uses
Organization website	Primary site used by organization	Used as primary location for incident info in small to medium events. Link to incident site for large.	Since used for routine business, caution in having it superseded by event info and traffic
Incident or "dark" site	Use to pre-stage information for maximum speed. Provide incident specific info off primary site.	Protects on-going business and site activity, protects primary site traffic. Properly staged greatly increases initial response speed	Primary location of response info. Social sites should drive traffic here. Best if on full-function management platform including contact and inquiry management
Email		A declining but still primary method of delivery info and messages to individuals	Important to pre-stage critical contacts for immediate email delivery.
Text Messages	Uses cell phone and cell data systems to deliver short (140 characters or less) messages	Primary means of emergency alerts. High value in alerts for public safety, also for new info notices	Text alerts for public warnings, notify press of events, alert opt-in groups to specific info availabilities. Two-way text can receive info from audiences
Automated Phone	Automated calling using text-to-voice conversions.	Supplement to text alerts as uses land and cell phones. Can carry more in-depth messages.	

RSS	Really Simple Syndication. Allows easy distribution of content to other sites	Facilitates automated distribution to other websites. High value when other organizations or related sites are involved.	Wider distribution of info to other websites and individuals through readers or aggregators
Widgets	Programming code that allows for presentation of content from your site on other sites	Similar to RSS but controls presentation	Easy re-distribution of content through other websites
Live Video/ Webcasts	Live video presented through incident site or streaming site such as Ustream or Livestream.	High value for transparency. May be required by government or public pressure.	Provide access to high interest activity. Also, present live events with leaders, subject matter experts. Can combine with live chat for real time interaction.
Twitter	Very common microblogging site, 140 characters or less. Used by almost all media as primary news source.	May be most important channel for crisis and emergency communication other than website. Primary means for media updates.	Provide "mini-updates" and alerts of new releases published on site

Facebook	Most popular social media channel with nearly 1 billion global users.	Very high importance in amplifying message through networks, and providing interactivity.	Simple posts of info, direct to website, encourage and manage questions and comments. Best used when interactivity consolidated on comm management platform.
Google+	Google competitor to Facebook. Advantages include easy video and tie to search engine	Growing in significance at publication time, but still limited.	Same as Facebook, addition of Circles to segment audiences and interest groups
Wikis and Wikipedia	Wikipedia is massive online encyclopedia and will include entries for all major events contributed by anyone. Wikis use same technology to create special interest "encyclopedia-style" sites	Wikipedia has extensive reach and influence so must be monitored and corrected if errors occur	Correct distribution of info, particularly for long term use. Wiki's provide additional means of distributing information-heavy content
YouTube	Massive video site for uploading and viewing videos.	Videos becoming a primary requirement of crisis comms. Audiences will search YouTube first for relevant videos.	Provide event info, key messages, wider access to press conferences and interviews. Important in countering rumors, attacks and misinformation

Vimeo	Alternative video site. Used more by video producers.	Hosting videos on YouTube or Vimeo expands audience and reduces bandwidth on website. Can embed on site.	Same as YouTube.
Pinterest	A social media channel focused on visual images and links—scrapbook style	As of this writing quickly emerging in significance, particularly among women	Used to display photos, provide links to additional info, help distribute key messages and info
Flickr	Popular site for uploading and viewing photos.	Increases access to photos and reduces bandwidth and site. Can deliver images via site.	Images for use by media and public to communicate response actions, leaders.
Blogs	Websites, such as Wordpress and Blogspot, designed for easy publishing and facilitating comments	Important if main site used does not provide easy posting or comments. Typically main site should have primary info.	Enables more detailed info than Facebook or Twitter.

Processing Raw Information

The first task of the Information Production unit is to review the event information that is being provided by the Information Gathering unit. Is it what is needed? Is it complete? Do you know the status in terms of verification or validation? An important task is to give guidance to the Information Gathering unit on the questions that are emerging and where additional information is needed. Close collaboration and a cooperative work environment is obviously very helpful.

No doubt there will be a lot of information that is of secondary importance. The unit must quickly sort through the details provided to get at the information that is most critical for processing. Clearly the plans, strategies and objectives as set forth by the Communication Lead and as monitored by the Team Manager should provide the guidance for making the prioritization decisions. If the directives provided are not clear enough to assist in those decisions, the Information Production Lead needs to talk this over with the Team Manager to get clarification.

Information Approval Process

Information Approvals

In this plan, the necessity of security approvals for information released falls on the Information Production unit. As this is one area of the plan fraught with challenge and risk, the Team Manager will be closely involved in making certain the proper processes are in place and the system is working properly.

Without question the most difficult challenge for crisis communication today is meeting the demands for instant information while also maintaining information discipline. By information discipline, I am referring to the necessity of securing approvals prior to release of information. That approval process should limit factual errors, help prevent unnecessary legal problems from emerging from public statements, help insure the right strategy and priority of communication, and help insure consistency of information and messaging across all elements of the organization and response. Looked at this way, the approval process is one of the most important aspects of the crisis communication plan. A wise and experienced Communication Lead will rely on this process to help protect the reputation of the organization, build trust and also protect their own future.

However, as we have discussed, information today waits for no one. It comes from the crowd and all possible sources, is instantly amplified by media and social media, and often erupts and disappears in cycles that are both intense and brief. That means an approval process that takes almost any time at all dooms most information and many messages to irrelevance before they can even be issued. Anyone involved in major incidents can point to numerous examples of important messages completely lost because the approval process dragged out longer than the media and public interest in the issue. The bottom line of communication today is: be fast or be irrelevant. There really is no middle ground here. So the question of critical importance is: how do you manage the approval process to secure the benefits of information discipline while at the same time avoid irrelevance through timely release.

This plan, as discussed earlier, is based on the National Incident Management System, the Incident Command System, and the widely used government communication protocol known as the Joint Information Center Model. This requires Incident Commander approval of all released information. Because the Incident Command function is provided by Unified Command in a large, multi-agency response, it may means as many as six individuals with authority over the release and all of them have the right to change, veto or delay the release. Clearly, this is very burdensome and results in traditional JIC processes being untenable in today's information environment.

Guidelines for Information Approvals

The following can serve as a guide in developing the procedures needed to deal with this very significant challenge.

Information discipline is essential

Some process for making certain factual information is verified, that policies are followed, that key messages are consistently presented and that information conforms to the directions given by response leaders and the Communication Lead is essential.

Speed is also essential

If the information approval process is too slow, the organization should realize that they can save money by sending the communication team home. Information that is released after the interest in it has passed has no relevance or value.

Much can be pre-approved

Much of the information needed in a response, particularly in the first minutes and hours, can be developed in advance, pre-approved and pre-staged. This includes Initial Statements to be used announcing an event. The Risk Matrix should be used as a guide and legal and executive approval secured for the template. Then the key facts can be added without requiring additional approval. Fact sheets, backgrounders, Q&A documents, inquiry answers and other information types can largely be pre-approved and pre-staged. Agreements should be made in advance of the scope permitted for changing the templates without requiring approvals.

Approvals of facts and key messages ONLY—no micro-managing or word-smithing allowed

The information discipline process should be focused on the major incident facts and key messages of the response leaders. Confirmation of major news worthy facts such as estimates of scope of the incident, injuries or fatalities, announcements of major plans and activities should all be subject to the approval process. This includes the specific expression of key messages of concern, commitment, changes in policy related to the incident, etc. That leaves much that needs to be left to the discretion of the Communication Lead. Tweets with updates of relatively minor facts, confirmation of items already well established, announcements of press conferences and meetings, release of new information on the website— these are the kind of items which should be left to the good judgment of the

Communication Lead and team. A response leader who requires that he or she needs to personally approve every document, every iteration of a message, and every fact is dooming the response communications to irrelevance and likely dooming the reputation of the organization even while doing his or her best to protect it.

Trust is essential

The only way for the information discipline and fast release requirements to be met is for a high degree of trust and confidence between the Communication Lead and the response leaders. The response leaders need to be confident that the Communication Lead understands and fully respects the need for approval of significant information releases. At the same time, he or she needs to be trusted by the response leaders to use good judgment, to know what can be safely released without approval, and to make certain that the credibility of the response team can never be question by the release of inaccurate information.

Work this out in advance

You simply cannot wait for a real event to determine how information discipline and approvals will be handled. It's a sure way to lose trust within the team even while losing trust with the media and the public. The process needs to be embedded in the organization's crisis and emergency response plans, it needs to include all key participants including attorneys and subject matter experts and it needs to drilled as part of the crisis exercises conducted by the organization.

Expanded Info Production team roles

For larger events, several team members will need to be assigned to the Information Production unit. The following provides guidance for individual roles:

Writer(s)

Despite the increase in visual communication in a crisis, writing is still at the heart of preparing information for release. Ideally writers will have considerable experience in journalistic writing and understand how to craft information with clarity, priority, and brevity. The ability to draft messages that meet the strategic direction of the Communication Lead and communicate with clarity and precision is necessary, as is the fastidious eye of an excellent editor. Despite the high urgency, even minor errors in fact and grammar can produce significant problems and loss of credibility.

Multi-Media Producer

In this plan we've grouped together all non-writing information production tasks under the Multi-Media Producer role. This includes photography, videography, graphic design, GIS/mapping, and presentation development. Clearly in larger events with high demand for multi-media, this team will include several members with different areas of expertise.

Of particular concern is for this team to have the necessary tools at their disposal in an event. That means sufficiently powerful and graphics oriented computers, software, cameras, editing systems, lights, map applications, and more. In some situations, such as industrial accidents where toxic material or fire and explosions are an issue, it may be necessary to have a Hazwopper trained photographer and videographer available. Frequently the sites of these kinds of incidents are closed to everyone except those with training and being able to provide images and video from the field for the media as well as for use on the incident website and social media is very important.

Special Needs Production

Frequently events involve individuals or populations that are non-English speaking. There may also be groups with functional disabilities that need to receive the information and cannot access it with traditional methods. The

Team Manager needs to assign a team member with background or expertise in communicating with non-English speaking language groups or functional disabilities. This person focus on those special needs populations, advising the Information Production Lead on special requirements and assuming the lead in developing the needed materials.

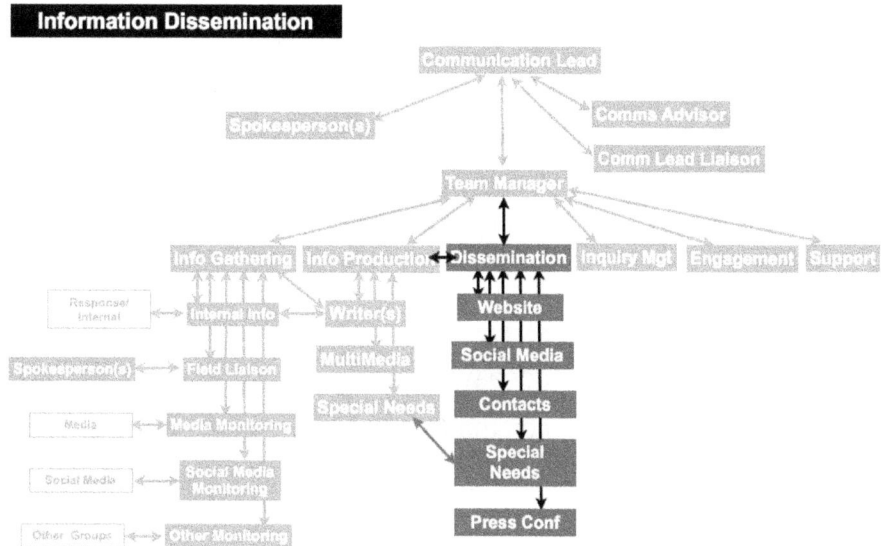

Dissemination Lead

The Dissemination Lead takes the approved information and distributes it to all audiences as directed by the Team Manager. Sometimes called the Channel Manager, this role is not typically found in media-centric crisis communication plans. If dissemination of approved information is based on providing press releases to the media by handout, email or snail mail, there is not much need for this role. But since crisis communication now involves setting up and maintaining multiple channels of communication aimed at multiple different audiences, groups, segments and individuals, the Dissemination Lead is rapidly evolving into one of the most significant roles on the team.

Information Discipline—last check

The Dissemination unit represents the last opportunity to make certain the information discipline process has been followed and that all necessary approvals have been secured. It remains the responsibility of Information Production to secure these approvals, a final confirmation before delivery will help insure that the process works.

Audiences and why to communicate directly

Audiences

The Dissemination unit is responsible for collecting, managing and maintaining audience contacts. This includes media contacts but goes far beyond that. Identifying the audiences you will need to communicate with during a crisis or emergency is an important task that fortunately can be done well before an event occurs. Unfortunately, if it is not done, the crisis communication team will not have the distinct advantage of communicating directly with the people who absolutely need to hear from you.

The ability of an organization to recover after a crisis, particularly a reputation crisis, is based primarily on the perception of those outside the response: customers, employees, investors, donors, taxpayers, regulators, neighbors, and so on. One of the most important exercises to do prior to an event is to identify the people whose opinion about your organization matters most for its future. In almost all cases where I have done that, it comes to a relatively small number of readily identifiable people. These people will decide on your future based on their perceptions of the character, competence and trust-worthiness of the leaders in a response. This being the case, why would you not want to communicate directly and interactively with these people when everything is on the line? Why would you even consider putting their perceptions and the future of your organization in the hands of others (media and social media commentators) whose primary objection is usually to attract an audience—even at your expense?

The following is a listing of potential audiences you should consider, why they are important, and challenges to securing and maintaining current contact information.

Audience	Why important	Contact sources	Comments
Media	"Message amplifiers" and a primary way many are informed and form opinions	Existing PR contacts, media data bases, wire services. During event website needs to allow media to join list for updates	The ability to capture, categorize and distribute to reporters is essential. Best practice is use of communication software allowing collaboration.
Internal Team	Keeping everyone involved in the response and organization leaders informed is essential to effective response	Organization employee lists	
Response Partners	Includes those involved directly or indirectly in a response. Might be hospital, Red Cross, gov agencies, volunteer organizations, etc.	Confer with emergency management to identify response participants. Likely requires individual identification and maintenance	Communicating with response partners, often ignored, is critical not only to trust but to effective response management
Employees	Employees have a right to the best possible, most direct information and their opinion will matter much after the event is over	Human Resources—either crisis comm team must have access or work closely with HR during event to deliver	Challenge in communicators accessing this list. May involve labor. May require decision at highest levels.

Employee Families	Employee family members crucial in forming opinions about organization	Usually an opt-in process, but should be done prior. System should allow self-maintenance	Opt-in reduces issues about organizational communication with families.
Customers	Opinions of customers, particularly key customers, of highest importance in recovery	Sales or marketing databases. Requires collaboration or automated maintenance.	Similar to employees may be closely held in "silo." If not controlled by crisis team, then holders of the contacts need to be included in Dissemination unit.
Industry Contacts	Small number of contacts may be inordinately influential	Marketing or business development.	
Investors & Donors	Similar to customers. Future of organization may depend on their perception.	Controlled by Investor or Donor Relations and legal issues involved. Close collaboration with IR required.	
Community Leaders	Opinion leaders in affected communities	Developed from community associations, web searches. Can create opt-in list as part of community relations plan.	Difficult to develop targeted list but essential in many events.
Fenceline Neighbors	Located nearest facilities. Potential source of legal issues and long term concern	Local community outreach	

Government Officials	Local, regional and national elected officials; regulatory agency staff	Readily available lists including internal from legal or regulatory affairs. May require collaboration with Gov Affairs department	Direct, honest communication can pay long term dividends
Activists and Opponents	Can defuse and diffuse opposition by direct communication	May exist from past activity. Capture and manage contacts during event	Often ignored but activism and strong opposition can be minimized by outreach, transparency.

Audiences and Release Timing

In a media-centric public relations world, the standard process for a major announcement or news release was to put it on the news wires, and then release to the public, customers, and even internal audiences. Many practitioners still think that way. Now, key individuals and groups have a much higher expectation of getting information directly from the organization. Employees, key customers, major investors and donors do not want to get information vital to them from the news media. When communicators understand the imperative of the news media to highlight fear and outrage to attract audiences in an attention-saturated world, they prefer to have these critical audiences get the information directly from them. Trusting the media to convey those messages is putting the future in the hands of those who have a very different, and often contrary, agenda.

The general rule is all audiences should receive the information simultaneously and the information should be completely consistent. While some audiences may require additional information of interest to them, what is provided must be completely consistent in information content and key messages because sharing and comparing is almost certain to happen and can be done almost instantaneously via the Internet. There are some circumstances where some audiences require advance release— government regulators may require advance release or internal executives may want some time to be alerted to major news announcements. But these are the exceptions to the general rule of simultaneous and consistent release.

The challenge is how this simultaneous release is to be accomplished. Here is where the web-based communication management technologies are very valuable because they provide contact management capabilities along with content management. All audiences can be incorporated into a single platform, often with automated updating from other sources such as HR software to maintain updated employee information. With a single action updates or releases can be published to the website and delivered by means of email, text messages or robo-call automated phone calling to all audiences. These can also be set to deliver messages to other websites via RSS feeds and widgets and control social media channels through connectors that allow instantaneous distribution.

If such a system is not available to the crisis communication team (and must be set up prior to an event), the options are to use the commonly available tools including standard email systems, email distribution applications, CRM systems, web content management systems, web-based collaborative apps, and so on. In many cases, as the audience chart above indicates, where the communicators do not have direct control over important audience contacts, it is essential that those who do have control are incorporated into the crisis communication team. If employee contacts are controlled only by HR, then authorized HR representatives must be closely connected to the team through the Dissemination Lead so that employees can receive virtually simultaneous updates. The same is true of customers, investors, government contacts, etc. This is often one of the most difficult challenges to overcome in preparing to respond because of the "silos" or fixed barriers between different departments. Personal conflicts and internal battles for control can significantly impact the willingness and ability to collaborate. This area of preparation may need high level leadership involvement to overcome the expected obstacles and resistance.

Communication Channels

Below is a list is some of the most important channels being used for crisis and emergency communication today. While this list may seem long compared to the single channel, mainstream media, that prevailed just a few short years ago, it is by no means exhaustive. Nor is it necessarily current as changes occur in this arena almost daily. It is essential that the communication team include a person or team members who are deeply involved in the changing technology of communications. One important role of the Dissemination Lead is to continually monitor and update the channels used.

Prioritization of channels to be used largely depends on the audiences and the event. The guiding principle needs to be to go where your audiences are going and that means the Dissemination Lead needs to be aware of the audiences' channel preferences. A note of caution: there are many false assumption about audience participation in the Internet, social media, and news sources. Many times uses are counter-intuitive. For example, one assumption may be that lower income groups, or non-English language groups may have considerably lower use of mobile Internet devices. These assumptions should be challenged and facts about use can be verified using resources such as the Pew Internet and American Life research studies.

Channel	Description	Importance	Uses

Organization website	Primary site used by organization	Used as primary location for incident info in small to medium events. Link to incident site for large.	Since used for routine business, caution in having it superseded by event info and traffic
Incident or "dark" site	Use to pre-stage information for maximum speed. Provide incident specific info off primary site.	Protects on-going business and site activity, protects primary site traffic. Properly staged greatly increases initial response speed	Primary location of response info. Social sites should drive traffic here. Best if on full-function management platform including contact and inquiry management
Email		A declining but still primary method of delivery info and messages to individuals	Important to pre-stage critical contacts for immediate email delivery.
Text Messages	Uses cell phone and cell data systems to deliver short (140 characters or less) messages	Primary means of emergency alerts. High value in alerts for public safety, also for new info notices	Text alerts for public warnings, notify press of events, alert opt-in groups to specific info availabilities. Two-way text can receive info from audiences
Automated Phone	Automated calling using text-to-voice conversions.	Supplement to text alerts as uses land and cell phones. Can carry more in-depth messages.	

RSS	Really Simple Syndication. Allows easy distribution of content to other sites	Facilitates automated distribution to other websites. High value when other organizations or related sites are involved.	Wider distribution of info to other websites and individuals through readers or aggregators
Widgets	Programming code that allows for presentation of content from your site on other sites	Similar to RSS but controls presentation	Easy re-distribution of content through other websites
Live Video/ Webcasts	Live video presented through incident site or streaming site such as Ustream or Livestream.	High value for transparency. May be required by government or public pressure.	Provide access to high interest activity. Also, present live events with leaders, subject matter experts. Can combine with live chat for real time interaction.
Twitter	Very common microblogging site, 140 characters or less. Used by almost all media as primary news source.	May be most important channel for crisis and emergency communication other than website. Primary means for media updates.	Provide "mini-updates" and alerts of new releases published on site

Facebook	Most popular social media channel with nearly 1 billion global users.	Very high importance in amplifying message through networks, and providing interactivity.	Simple posts of info, direct to website, encourage and manage questions and comments. Best used when interactivity consolidated on comm management platform.
Google+	Google competitor to Facebook. Advantages include easy video and tie to search engine	Growing in significance at publication time, but still limited.	Same as Facebook, addition of Circles to segment audiences and interest groups
Wikis and Wikipedia	Wikipedia is massive online encyclopedia and will include entries for all major events contributed by anyone. Wikis use same technology to create special interest "encyclopedia-style" sites	Wikipedia has extensive reach and influence so must be monitored and corrected if errors occur	Correct distribution of info, particularly for long term use. Wiki's provide additional means of distributing information-heavy content
YouTube	Massive video site for uploading and viewing videos.	Videos becoming a primary requirement of crisis comms. Audiences will search YouTube first for relevant videos.	Provide event info, key messages, wider access to press conferences and interviews. Important in countering rumors, attacks and misinformation

Vimeo	Alternative video site. Used more by video producers.	Hosting videos on YouTube or Vimeo expands audience and reduces bandwidth on website. Can embed on site.	Same as YouTube.
Pinterest	A social media channel focused on visual images and links—scrapbook style	As of this writing quickly emerging in significance, particularly among women	Used to display photos, provide links to additional info, help distribute key messages and info
Flickr	Popular site for uploading and viewing photos.	Increases access to photos and reduces bandwidth and site. Can deliver images via site.	Images for use by media and public to communicate response actions, leaders.
Blogs	Websites, such as Wordpress and Blogspot, designed for easy publishing and facilitating comments	Important if main site used does not provide easy posting or comments. Typically main site should have primary info.	Enables more detailed info than Facebook or Twitter.

Crisis dark sites

When an event of high interest happens, audiences of all kinds will come to your organization directly for information. Any website or social media channel used by your organization will likely see massively increased traffic. This is one of the main reasons to have a crisis dark site that is hosted separately from your primary website or sites. Hosting needs to be on very robust servers, preferably with geographic redundancy and proven reliability. A crisis site can literally receive millions of page views per day and if it hosts images, video, live video and heavy graphics the bandwidth requirements may be very high.

Best practice is to have a crisis dark site on a full-function communication management platform. These include the ability to manage content, push out messages through multiple channels including social media, manage audience contacts, allow audience opt-in to email lists and text messages, manage the inquiries and interactions and provide automated summaries and reports. If this is not possible, at the minimum the crisis dark site has to allow for very rapid changes of information fully controlled by the communication team without requiring a "webmaster" or specially trained IT technicians. But, having technical staff with deep experience in web-based communication of all kinds is almost a necessity on any crisis communication team and these people would be part of the Dissemination unit in this plan.

Audience Opt-In

If the systems you are using do not allow visitors coming to your sites to add themselves to a mailing list, you will have a lot of extra and unnecessary work to do. While this requirement has been lessened by the widespread use of social media, there are still many individuals who would like to get email and/or text updates about the incident. As mentioned above, communication management systems incorporate this important feature and automate the process saving much time. However, commonly available systems such as MailChimp, ConstantContact and many others can also be used. As with all technologies, these must be implemented and tested prior to an incident for maximum effectiveness.

Expanded Team Assignments

The expanded plan calls for several team members to take responsibility for different aspects of Dissemination.

Website Specialist—primary focus the site or sites where incident information is presented including insuring that all interactive functions are working properly. A person with a strong technical orientation is valuable.

Social Media Specialist—for larger events a sizeable team under a designated leader will likely be required to manage the various social media channels used. Close coordination with Inquiry Management unit is necessary in effectively managing the interactions.

Contact Specialist—person or team designated to manage the audience contacts, create appropriate lists for email, text (or even snail mail). This person manages the process of incorporating the information from those who wish to be added to email or text distribution lists.

Special Needs Distribution—works closely with the Special Needs Production specialist in making certain that all special needs individuals and groups are receiving the information they need.

Press Conference Coordinator—since this plan includes distribution of content to the media as part of Dissemination, press interviews and press conferences are a primary way of distributing information to the press. This person, working closely with Support, provides the planning, coordination and management of major press interviews and press conferences.

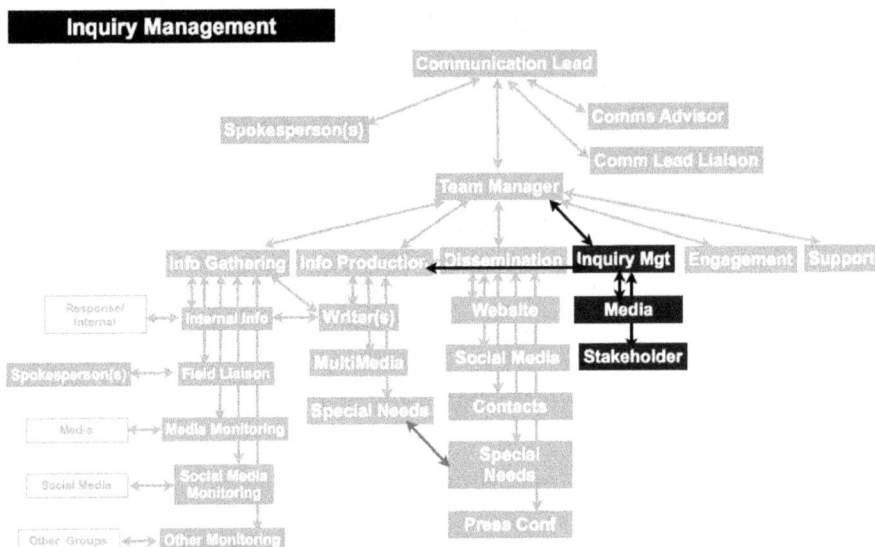

Inquiry Management

Inquiry Management Lead

The task of the Inquiry Management unit is to manage all the interactions from those coming to your organization through the website(s), social media channels, phone calls, emails, text messages and other channels. This unit does not manage the interactions that are part of press interviews and press conferences but does make certain that those interactions are documented and recorded as part of the documentation and reporting function. Similarly, this unit does not manage the personal interactions with stakeholders done by the Engagement unit, but does insure that those interactions are also documented and incorporated into inquiry and interaction reports.

In many ways, direct interaction with individuals is the heart of today's crisis communication. As stated so often here already, crisis communication is not about delivering messages to the media who deliver to multiple audiences. Crisis communication is about direct interaction with multiple individuals who make up those audiences. In major events, these interactions can literally be thousands per hour.

Managing inquiries has long been an important part of crisis management. In traditional plans a call center may be set up specifically for handling media calls. The JIC Model has a function for responding to phone calls from the media. Other interactions such as questions from customers may be handled by a customer service call center. Questions from employees or families may be handled by the HR department. Questions received via interviews or press conferences were disconnected from the phone inquiries unless call center staff attended the conferences. Questions from response partners, in an ICS and JIC event, were sent to the Liaison Officer—not even part of the communication team. Everything was recorded on scraps of paper or not recorded at all limiting the use of all these interactions in quickly responding to issues or forming plans and strategies.

Why answer questions from all audiences?

This plan takes a different approach by consolidating all audience interactions with one group and assuming web-based and collaborative technologies are used to interact with audiences and record, manage and facilitate all interactions. This is important for these reasons:

Reduce phone calls – most inquiries and interactions are now through websites, web forms, social media channels, email and text messages. The phone is still important but much less so than it used to be. Reporters and many others rely more on Twitter to get the latest information.

Fast, consistent information—if the job of managing inquiries is spread across many different groups and locations it is very difficult if not impossible to make certain that everyone is receiving the best available and consistent information. A very good way to upset people, like employees, customers and investors, is for them to find out that when they called they got a very different story, or a much later update than others did.

Interactions are vital for monitoring—one of the best ways to know what issues are emerging, what new questions are popping up and what rumors or misinformation is getting legs, is to monitor the interactions.

Frequently this is where vital response information initiates. It is also where communication and response leaders can gain valuable sentiment and trend information so necessary for ongoing communication strategy. But if this information is disconnected, and not accessible to communication team leaders on a near real-time basis, the value is largely lost.

Interactions are not just about questions—audiences use these interactive channels not just to ask questions but for a variety of purposes. Many wish to volunteer or to make suggestions for how response managers can deal with a response. The emergence of social networking has meant that in major events hundreds to even millions of citizens get involved in information sharing, in helping victims find family members, water and other needed resources. It's also true that in some events many take to blogs, crowd-sourced news sites like Digg and Reddit, and comment opportunities on the crisis site or organization's social media channels to express their perspectives and opinions—often in extreme, rude and vulgar terms. This means that training for Inquiry Management is not simply a matter of helping team members get approved information in answer to questions. It is far more complex and challenging than that, which means it makes sense to consolidate the team members who need to go through that training into a single group.

Technology to support interactive management

Inquiry Management technology

Inquiry management has moved far beyond setting up a phone bank to answer an anticipated flood of media calls. The Internet has made brought interaction management to the forefront and it is virtually impossible to effectively manage the massive influx of direct interactions with large numbers of important stakeholders without using sophisticated technology. Best practice is to use special purpose web-based communication management systems designed specifically for this purpose. These allow questions and comments from many different channels including the website(s), phone, email, text, and social media channels to be consolidated into a central, virtual control center. These also allow automated distribution of interactions through email to designated responders, subject matter experts, or communication team leaders. These systems also allow the Inquiry Management team to be geographically dispersed as all tools and information needed are available on the web-based control center.

An important feature of these platforms is the ability to quickly produce and share approved information and answers with the Inquiry Management team. Some allow approved answers to be selected from a pull-down menu which then fills in the response box for very efficient responses.

If your organization is not using such systems and has no plans to invest in them, there are other options to consider including creating dedicated applications through technologies such as Sharepoint or Drupal. Using collaborative tools such as Google Docs with the spreadsheet application to log and track inquiries. Forcing all interactions onto a minimum of widely used channels such as Facebook or Twitter. Using web forms in conjunction with the your organization's or crisis site. Developing a crisis site using blog tools such as Wordpress which have large numbers of plug-ins, some of which may be adapted for this purpose.

Guidelines for the Inquiry Management Lead

Approved information only

While everyone may subscribe to the idea of using only approved information, at the Inquiry Management unit level the rubber really meets the road. That's because the team members here are continually interacting directly with those outside the response including reporters, bloggers, stakeholders, response partners, impacted citizens and the like. As mentioned before, it is from these people that much valuable information about the response may be gained—information that may not be known by the response team. More about that below. But this also means that the

Inquiry responders may be the first to know clearly established facts as well as rumors and unverified information. It is very tempting to not confirm these facts with other inquirers, and it is difficult for a responder to say: "We understand that information is being reported by others but we have not been able to confirm it at this time." When the information in question is already well established through other channels, it makes the responder and response team look out of touch and impossibly slow if confirmation of well established facts is not very fast in coming.

This is one important reason why the Communication Lead needs to have delegated authority to approve the release of facts and information when such information has been clearly established. It is also why it is essential, even for information which must go through the full approval process, that the process be as simple and streamlined (read fast!) as possible.

Despite this issue, maintaining information discipline is still very important and the Inquiry Management team may need to be reminded of how much of a problem can be created by communicating unapproved information.

Monitoring and team interaction

Because so much valuable information about the event, rumors and public sentiment is gained through the interactions of the Inquiry Management unit, this information must get as quickly as possible to those who need it for their jobs. Some of the information is invaluable for the response leaders and the appropriate channel is through the Communication Lead who will be in continual contact with the Team Manager. Some is essential for the Information Gathering Lead or one of the groups within this unit such as social media monitoring. This additional information needs to be incorporated into monitoring reports provided by the Information Gathering unit. There must be direct interaction between those Inquiry Management team members and team members or leaders of these units. The Engagement also interacts directly with stakeholders so the coordination and collaboration with team members in both units is essential for full situation awareness.

The lines of authority over these units still should be clear. But the lines of authority and reporting responsibilities should not hinder the free flow of information between others on the team who need the information.

If communication management technology is used or other collaborative tools, this sharing of information can be significantly enhanced while improving speed and efficiency.

Set inquiry response goals

Responding promptly to inquiries, comments and suggestions is a necessity simply because audiences today expect that. Reporters have little patience for delayed response and will simply turn to other sources. Similarly, individuals with pressing questions ("When will my power come back on? Or "Who do I call for info of lost loved ones?") have little patience for responses that come hours or even days later.

Response time goals may vary with volume of inquiries, but a two-hour minimum response time is reasonable under most circumstances. Some responses may take more time due to the nature of the question. The Inquiry Management Lead should work closely with Support Lead to make certain adequate staff to meet the demand are available. Coverage for longer duration events including transition time is critical. Communication management systems can track response time and other metrics automatically. If such systems are not used, other systems used to track inquiries such as spreadsheets or database programs should include the time they arrive, whether or not they are pending or in progress, and when they are completed.

Use of Subject Matter Experts

Responding accurately to questions may include using Subject Matter Experts (SMEs). These may include members of the legal team, technical or engineering experts, human resource personnel, traffic manager, logistics specialists or any number of specialties represented in your event. Building a list of SMEs with current contact information is one of the best things to do to prepare. The SMEs are members of the team so need to be included in the collaborative interaction response systems or technologies used.

Pre-staging Answers

Time spent in responding to inquiries can be greatly reduced by pre-staging inquiry answers before an event. It is well established that about 75% of the questions asked during an event can be anticipated in advance. That means that answers can be crafted, reviewed and approved prior to an event occurring. This reduces response time and greatly reduces the workload in the critical early hours of a major event.

Not all questions can be anticipated as the event itself will generate unanticipated issues or concerns. But developing answers to emerging questions when it becomes clear that the volume of questions will warrant it is a certain way to stay ahead of the game. If the answer goes beyond approved information or messages then it must be approved prior to use. Systems used to manage inquiries sometimes have functions built in to provide answers in easy to access form and which instantly populate an email back to the inquirer. If these systems are not used, more general tools such as Google Docs can help provide answer documents to be used by the team, even if they are geographically dispersed.

How and why to work to minimize inquiries

As seen from the expanded organization chart, the Inquiry Management team will quickly grow to the largest unit of the response. In some events where many communities and high levels of public interest are involved, the Engagement unit may become bigger, but this would be only for certain types of events. The primary goal of Inquiry Management unit is to quickly, accurately and appropriately respond to all inquiries, comments, suggestions and personal expressions. Doing this can encourage a higher volume because reporters and stakeholders may find they can get the information they want best by calling, sending an email or texting. However, this is contrary to a second major goal of the unit which is to reduce the number of interactions—particularly questions.

Questions (unlike expressions of support or outrage) are generated because the inquirer wants information. If the information they seek is provided, there is no need for questions. A high volume of inquiries is a strong indication not just of high media and/or public interest, but a lack of information. This is one important reason why the Communication Lead and Team Manager need to track inquiry volumes very closely, and why the Inquiry Management Lead needs to report on changes in volume to the Team Manager. This is also why the Inquiry Management Lead needs to confer frequently with the Information Gathering Lead and the Information Production Lead so they can be gathering and producing the information that the inquirers are seeking.

Experienced crisis communication managers monitor inquiries very closely for emerging issues, rumors and information gaps. As soon as a trend is identified, information should be prepared and disseminated as far as is reasonable. Proactive pushing of the required information as well as making it readily accessible on the website will reduce call volume, according to some experienced communicators, by as much as two thirds.

Expanded team responsibilities

The OnePage expanded organization structure identifies two positions for the expanded team: Media Inquiries Lead and Stakeholder Inquiries Lead. This distinction is provided because there are special skills and experience involved in responding to reporters. However, in actual events the specifics of the event may require different divisions of responsibilities. For example, there may be multiple locations where team members are assigned and regional leads may be required. Also, it may be advisable to organize your team according to types of inquiries. If there are large numbers requiring technical expertise to answer or high levels of extremely negative comments, special teams may be assigned to those categories after receiving specific training or directions.

The Engagement Lead manages the team assigned to communicate in face-to-face settings with stakeholders. The focus is on victims and families, communities and community groups, and government officials including elected leaders, staff and agency personnel. The direct and personal interaction of response leaders and representatives of the response team with key individuals and groups has proven to be one of the most significant activities of the crisis communication team. Effective and sensitive interaction reduces legal action, speeds the organization and victims toward recovery and does much to protect, enhance or rebuild damaged reputations.

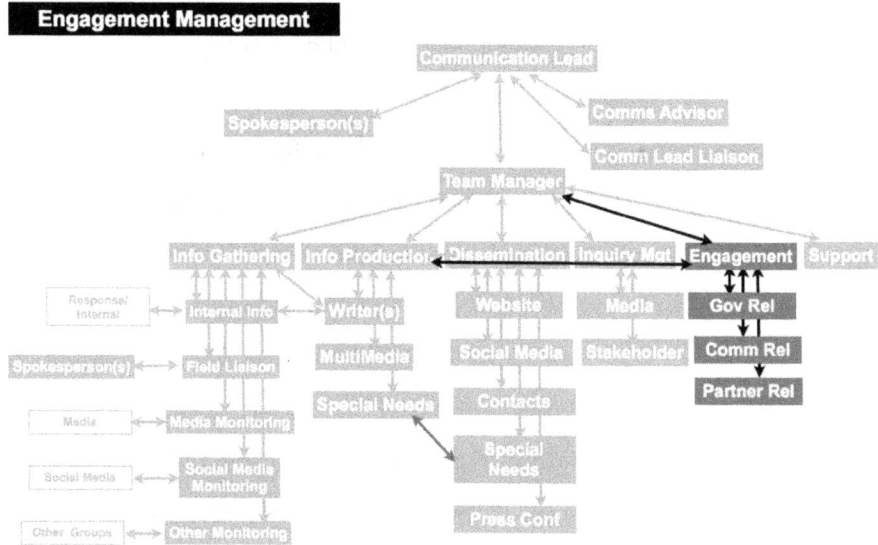

Engagement Lead

The Engagement unit is not included in many plans, consequently this is an area where many organizations fail. The reason is typically that the organization has people and departments who in normal times interact with key individuals and groups including communities and governments. The reporting relationships of those managers or groups do not typically go through the person designated in a response as the Communication Lead so when they are told during a very important crisis that they are now part of an overall team led by someone who is not normally their supervisor and may be lower in the organization, there is understandable resistance. Like other such obstacles, institutional and political resistance must be overcome prior to an event to prevent such problems from interfering in the response.

Engagement Audiences

Here we are focusing primarily on community, government and response partners. However, different events require different audience engagement priorities. Employees and their families may be a priority in certain events, while customers, investors, or neighbors next to a plant or facility may be most important in others. The Communication Lead must set the priority on audiences, groups and individuals on which to focus.

The addition of Response Partners to the engagement list may raise some questions. Response partners include government agencies involved in a response but without a representative in the Command Center, hospitals, Red Cross, volunteer groups, technical consultants and others actively involved. In an Incident Command Response, one of the three members of the Command Staff is the Liaison Officer. This person has the responsibility of working with all response partners who are not participating as members of Unified Command. However, this position was envisioned during a different era of public information and many events of the past decade using ICS have demonstrated the weakness of this element of ICS. Failures of the response organization to keep other affected government leaders and response organization leaders who are not co-located with the response team fully informed has damaged the response and generated much public criticism. Best practice today is to include response partners in the category of critical individuals and groups to keep fully informed of response activities. Incorporating them fully into lists for updates and designating team members to engage them directly will help prevent the problems experienced in these events.

Which individuals and groups to engage? In one sense, everyone is of equal importance and the communication effort overall must recognize that. That's why there is so much emphasis on direct communication via website, email, opt-in lists, and social media. But, in large events, not everyone can be engaged personally in face-to-face contacts. Prioritization should consider these elements:

- Influencers—who are the individuals or groups who would have maximum influence over the perceptions of other key audiences and individuals?

- Role—some by virtue of the role, job title or public position they hold can be very influential
- Personality—some groups and individuals can be much "louder" than others and therefore have an outsize effect on reputation or trust.
- Credibility—those individuals or groups considered to be highly credible by your target audiences should be included
- Longer term contacts—engagement as a process looks to the long term, not merely the immediate issues. In selecting individuals or groups the long term impact on the future of the organization needs to be considered.

Why engage?

Why engage?

There are three main goals of engagement:

1) demonstrate care and concern

2) listen for and respond to concerns, issues, questions and recommendations

3) make certain key groups and individuals get accurate and complete information.

Engagement should always been included as part of the response when trust would enhanced by personal interaction with individuals whose opinions about the organization will significantly impact its future. That means almost every event of consequence.

Care and concern is demonstrated most clearly by the actions taken by the response or organization leaders, but also by the effort to reach out to those with whom your are engaging. A caution: listening communicates respect, concern and empathy far more than providing information does. It's natural to think the whole idea of engagement is to speak at these important people. But the primary focus is listening and by listening carefully, responding, and helping them be a part of the response you will demonstrate care and concern for them in a very tangible way.

Listening guidelines

Here are some guidelines to help the Engagement team be successful in listening to its audiences:

Select for listening skills

Since listening is a skill, often in-born, sometimes learned, team members in the Engagement unit need to be considered for their listening skills.
Use multiple forms
There are many different ways to listen. The primary focus of the Engagement unit is active listening as part of face-to-face individual meetings, however other forms including surveys, web-forms, shopping mall interviews, establishing "listening posts" can also be used. The non-face-to-face methods are the responsibilities of the Information Gathering unit so close coordination is necessary to avoid overlap or duplication.

Come with questions

While in most situations the individuals or groups may be eager to communicate their concerns, questions and suggestions, it is best to come prepared to any meeting with questions you would like to raise with them. Simply saying: "I have some questions for you" makes it clear your intention is to listen and not just talk.

Commit to respond and actually respond

While you cannot control the actions or priorities of the response leaders in responding to the concerns or suggestions of the individuals or groups, you can commit to making certain response leaders hear of the concern and you can commit to getting back to your stakeholders with additional information or a decision of the leaders. The goodwill that is built by listening is quickly lost when it is seen that suggestions, questions or comments deemed important by them fall into a "black hole" without response or reaction.

Feed back what you heard

One of the most important disciplines of active listening is to tell the person or group you are listening to what you heard. This should be done by way of confirmation: "I heard this from you, is my understanding correct?" This prevents potential misunderstandings and demonstrates to them that you are listening carefully and fully intending to take action based on what you heard.

Guidelines for private meetings

Private Meetings

Many, if not most, of the interactions with individuals and groups will be in private, personal meetings. This may range from the President of the United States, to local elected officials, to major customers to family members of victims. Many will be initiated by the Engagement unit based on the strategy and priority of the Communication Lead. Others will be at the request of the individuals or groups. A few guidelines:

Approved information and messages—do not allow the confidential nature of these meetings to cause loss of information discipline. Revelation of information not available as part of the updates must be approved by the Communication Lead and/or the response leadership.

Everything is on the record—while you may be assured of full confidentiality, what is said and how it is said must be considered to be fully transparent to those outside the room.

Attitude—It may be difficult in protracted events to lose sight of the nature and impact of the event. Organizations in the crosshairs need to work to avoid defensiveness and to avoid communicating arrogance, lack of humility or impatience.

Guidelines for public meetings

Public Meetings

In some events it will be necessary to hold public meetings as part of the engagement process. These can be challenging if the event has inflamed emotions or if the issues involved are likely to draw out activist groups.

Here are some guidelines:

Locations--Choosing locations that are convenient for those attending is important. It may be hard to estimate the size needed be erring on the side of choosing a larger room is valuable. A packed room sends a message that you were not prepared for the interest and can heighten tensions and emotions.

Security--Security is essential and in sufficient force to handle a worst-case scenario. Security should be not be highly visible but should become visible quickly if the situation requires it.

Facilitator--Facilitation of public meetings with high emotions or tensions is a special skill and the facilitator should be carefully selected. While senior leaders, the CEO, Board Chairman, elected leaders or agency heads may be in attendance and participate, it is preferable to allow others to facilitate the meeting. Safety and security precautions should provide for a safe exit for the leaders should that be necessary.

Coordination with Inquiry Management Unit

The Engagement unit is not the only part of the crisis communication team to interact with stakeholders. The difference is the Engagement unit interacts primarily in face-to-face settings in individual, group and public meetings. The Inquiry Management unit interacts with those same stakeholders but through digital communications or phone calls. Certainly it is possible to focus the management of the interactions with stakeholders in one place, say the Community Relations section of the Engagement unit. This plan does not do that for the reasons outlined in the Inquiry Management section in this plan. Concentrating digital interactions with one group has some advantages. But, it depends on a high level of coordination with the Engagement unit.

Part of this coordination includes using the same communication management technology and control mechanisms to record and track interactions as used by the Inquiry Management unit. By concentrating all interactions in one place easily accessible to managers and assigned team members, monitoring and reporting become much easier.

Expanded team assignments

This plan envisions creating three sub-units for major events: community, government and response partners. A leader would be assigned to each of these units. This should be used as a general guide and other organization structures may be required. For example, if meeting with employees or family members, or family members of victims, is a big part of a response, team members designated for that difficult task may be organized into a unit. Span of control is important, however, and as the engagement team expands making certain that no one is responsible for more than seven direct reports will help with management tasks.

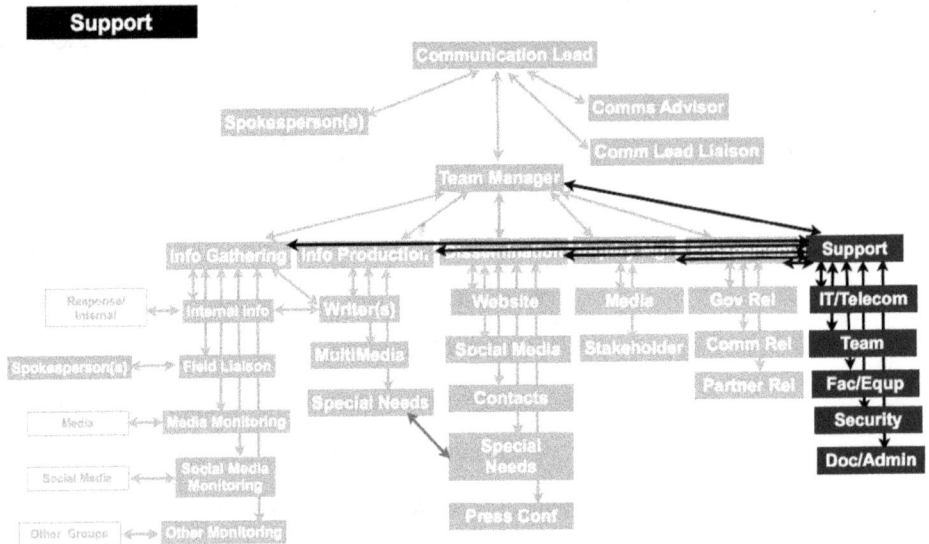

Support Lead

The role of the Support Lead is to make certain that the effectiveness of the entire crisis communication team and operation is not hindered by lack of resources. This requires continual review and assessment with the unit leaders and close collaboration with the Communication Lead and the Team Manager. It also means continually looking ahead to how the situation may escalate and how it may be extended in order to plan for resources that may be needed. Resources may be organized into the following categories:

Staffing and Team Needs
Facilities
Equipment, IT & Technology
Supplies
Security

Staffing and Team Needs

The people making up the team are the most important factor in determining whether the communication effort will be successful or not. Both quantity and quality matter. Advance planning in identifying the people who will be needed for worst case scenarios and extended events will significantly improve the quality of the response. Including at least the major players in all drills and exercises will also result in much more effective response.

Team needs include all of the items below, but here refer specifically to human and personal needs including food, bathroom facilities and rest space. Establishing reasonable shifts and length of duty without a break away from the event is very important to maintain the quality of the response. Everyone, including the Communication Lead, is replaceable. Since many large events today are global in nature involving media and audiences around the world, a 24/7 schedule will likely have to be maintained, at least during the intensive phase of the response. Shifts should be limited to 12 hours with length of duty no more than two weeks without a break of at least two days.

Facilities

The team needs adequate workspace, although the requirements are changing as web technology makes virtual response both a possibility and necessity. Dispersed teams with access to web-networked systems can work from any strong Internet connection. Meeting and working space is still essential.

Guidelines for facilities

A few guidelines:

Coordination with response leaders — it should be close, but not too close. Response leaders need to be able to meet and plan without interference. But the workspace of the communication team should be convenient in part because of the dual role played by the Communication Lead. The greater the distance, the more important the role of Communication Lead Liaison (or "runner") becomes.

Open plan and meeting space—ideally the workspace would provide for workstations with laptops or desktop computers in an open space configuration to support collaboration. If all units cannot fit into one space, the coordination between groups described in this plan should be used to help determine which units should be grouped in the same space. If an open room is used, closed meeting space should be provided for team leads to meet in private and for private conversations with unit leads and team members.

Media space--Press interview, press conference and public meeting space also needs to be provided, usually through the Support Lead. Press interview space can be more flexible, but special attention should be paid to acoustics, noise and visual distractions for video interviews. Arrangements need to be made for appropriate backdrops or visual settings. Press conference space is more challenging. Facility should be relatively convenient for response leaders to go between the conference space and their command center, but not too close to allow media interference with response management. It should be convenient for reporters and allow for adequate parking nearby including for satellite trucks. Acoustics, background visuals, and use of supporting visuals such as maps and graphics should be considered. Entry should be controlled for credentialed participants. Ideally, a meeting space off the main press conference space should be provided to allow participants to meet to prepare and debrief. Similar to public meeting space, the room should be more than adequate for the anticipated participants as extra room is better than one filled to capacity. The Support Lead may also be asked to provide space for public meetings, discussed under Engagement Lead.

Technology &
Equipment

Equipment, IT & Technology

Current communication technology is as essential to an effective response today as a well-crafted press release was for yesterday's response. Here is a brief list:

Electrical connections and backup power—Sufficient places to plug in including places to plug in cell phones, battery chargers, printers and other equipment. Backup power to entire workspace is very important.

Computers—a current computer is essential for almost all crisis communication team members.

Internet connection—sufficient bandwidth to support the entire team high speed access is essential. Redundancy should be built-in as loss of access for more than a few minutes may well prove devastating.

TV monitors with cable and DVD—very useful for viewing live cable broadcasts, also for presenting visual reports produced on DVD.

Data projectors—Projectors are essential for press conferences and public meetings, but the communication team itself needs several projector in the work areas and meeting rooms to effectively share information.

Printers and Scanners—Printers always seem to be in short supply. High speed printer should be available for larger jobs and printers in work areas shared by a few team members is ideal. Printer/scanner combinations will be adequate for most purposes but high quality scanners may be needed.

Crisis-capable servers—the crisis site used as the primary dissemination point should be hosted on servers separate from the organization and on a highly reliable, secure and geographically redundant system.

Telecommunications—cell phones have rapidly displaced the need for extensive phone banks and virtual call centers are emerging that allow for a single number to be published to connect to multiple cell phones in designated order. Planning should recognize the strong potential for loss of cell phone service in case of large-scale public event such as earthquake, severe weather and flooding. Satellite phones are now available that can provide a higher level of continuity at reasonable cost. If web-based communication management systems are used, continuity of operations in communication can be maintained through satellite phone connection to team members located outside of the affected area to operate the communication system. Conference line should also be available for the crisis communication team.

Radios—the emergency response team may rely on radios to maintain communication among the team. One or two radios need to be assigned to the communication function to allow access to information and contact with responders.

Communication management platform—Many organizations have adopted special-purpose web-based communication management system that consolidate virtually all crisis communication operations on a single, web-based control center. If such a system is not used, various other technologies such as Google Docs, web forms, content management systems and contact management systems need to be developed to meet the specific requirements identified throughout this plan.

Social media channels—Channels such as Facebook and Twitter will be a critically important part of the response and need to be established well in advance of any event. Ideally, interactions and content for these multiple channels will be managed through the communication management system mentioned above.

Video and Photography—Video and still cameras need to be used by the team and multiple means of delivering this content. Live video streaming is becoming an essential element. Numerous web services are available for publishing images (Flickr, Picasa), videos (YouTube, Vimeo), and live streaming real time video (Ustream, livestream, Bambuser). These channels need to incorporated through html embedded code into the crisis website to eliminate the need for visitors to go to multiple sites to get information they need.

Monitoring systems—the Information Gathering Lead section in this plan identifies the monitoring that must be done and some of the systems available. Many monitoring tools are available but are limited. As social media and Internet monitoring has become an essential part of basic public relations activities, the organization likely is using tools that will be effective during an event. If not, securing such services is an essential part of planning.

Software—Basic software for word processing, creating presentations, emailing and producing spreadsheets is, of course, essential. But special purpose software for geographic information, for managing images and video, for producing graphics is also essential. The Information Production requirements will provide a guideline for identifying the software needed and team members assigned to the Writer, Multi-Media Producer and Special Needs Production roles should be consulted for needs and preferences.

Photocopiers—yes, photocopiers are still an essential part of efficient operations. Fax machines? Not so much.

Supplies

Standard office supplies are necessary for efficient operations. These include paper, pens, paper clips, staplers, felt pens, scissors, file folders, expandable file folders, file cabinets or banker's boxes. Paper pads are useful for taking notes and copier paper should be in good supply. Three ring binders and paper punches are also often useful. White boards and dry-erase markers are an essential element. Flip charts and markers are often frequently used items and ideally come equipped with adhesive chart pads to allow for posting around the workspace. If the walls do not lend themselves to projection with the data projectors, then screens of some kind should be available. Maps of affected areas are important and appropriate maps based on the event scenarios can be stored for use during an event.

Checklist for Support

Category	Item	Quantity	Comments
Staff & Needs	Staff	Double complete team requirements for max shifts of 12 hrs, and duty tour of 2 week.	Plan for worst case scenario, escalation and long duration
	Food		Keeping team well supplied with healthy food a key to morale and performance
	Rest space		Quiet room nearby for brief rest
	Weather protection	Warm coats, umbrellas, rain gear	
Facilities	Team work space(s)	Spaces suitable for full Red team	Ideally with open plan, near but not with response leaders
	Team meeting space	For up to 10 team members	Separate from but near team work space

	Press interview locations	Appropriate location at office or on event site—wherever reporters may gather	Convenient to work space, chosen for good audio recording and appropriate visual background
	Press conference location(s)	Sufficient size to avoid overcrowding	Consider presentation area, multi-media set up, convenient for reporters, Satellite truck parking, away from but near response team, "green room for preparation, acoustics, background and security
	Public meeting facilities	Sufficient to avoid overcrowding	Convenient for community, adequate parking.
Equipment, IT & Technology	Computers	One for each member, spares	Laptops are very useful for mobility for meetings, and flexibility re the workspace
	Printers	High speed for large volume printing, plus several for work teams	
	Scanners	One high quality scanner sufficient	Printer/scanner combinations adequate for most uses

	Electrical outlets and backup power	Consider need for cell phone recharging as well as computers, printers, copiers, etc.	
	Internet connection	High speed & reliable	
	Data projectors	Meeting room, plus at least one for most units.	Very important for info sharing particularly for monitoring, viewing drafts, reports
	Crisis-capable web hosting	Crisis site on outside hosting, high bandwidth, redundant	
	TV monitor with cable, DVD	Monitoring unit and meeting room	Not essential but can be useful in tracking live coverage, also visual reports
	Cell phones with texting	Team members typically provide their own. Confirm use prior to event.	Texting is essential as it is more resilient than voice on cell networks, plus adds vital channel for internal comms
	Call center	30 phones typical for large scale response.	Virtual call center allows use of cell phones without requiring separate phone bank of landlines.
	Conference bridge		Conference line available designated for crisis communication team

	Radios	2-3 radios required if used by response team for primary internal comms	
	Communication management technology	System selected should not use seat-based pricing to allow team to fully participate	Web-based communication mgt system enable virtual team operations, maximum efficiency
	Social media channels		Continually in flux, but standards today are: Twitter, YouTube, Facebook, Flickr, Google+, Wordpress
	HD Digital SLR cameras	Ideally 2 cameras per major event site	Combined SLR/video ideal
	HD video cameras		
	Monitoring systems	If using subscription services adequate seats for monitoring unit	Free options include Google Alerts, Twitscoop, Tweetdeck, etc. Numerous subscription services available.
	Office software	Standard on all computers	Word, Excel, PowerPoint, Access or equivalents
	Graphics, image management and video editing software		Photoshop, InDesign, Pixelmator, iMovie, Final Cut, or equivalents. Video compression.
	Photocopiers	At least two including one high volume	One high volume and printer/scanner/copiers for units

Supplies	Paper and pens		Notepads plus copier paper
	File folders and expandable file		
	File cabinets or banker's boxes		
	White boards with markers	One per unit plus meeting room	
	Flip charts with markers, adhesive flip board paper	At least one per unit, plus meeting room	
	Screens or white walls for projectors		Large white paper can be assembled
	Maps		Based on event scenarios, plasticized for protection and marking
	Calendar		Plasticized large calendar for planning
	Staplers, paper clips		
	Binders		Always useful
	Paper punch		
	Sticky notes		
	Paper shredder		

Coordination with Logistics, Finance and Administration

Tracking costs and maintaining control over ordering of necessary resources are important but often overlooked parts of crisis communications. In ICS events, there are two sections involved: Logistics and Finance and Administration, both of which are primary operating units under Command. Logistics is responsible for planning for, ordering and securing delivery of all needed resources. Finance and Administration tracks costs, insures compliance with proper ordering, and reports to Command on current and projected response costs. Your organization's crisis or emergency response plan likely has components that related to Logistics and Finance and it is essential that the Support Lead understand what those requirements are and comply with them in meeting the needs of the crisis communication team.

If organizational processes are not well established, a web-based cost tracking application can be used, or a simple spreadsheet used to plan and keep track of what has been ordered and delivered.

Expanded team assignments

IT/Telecommunications Specialist—assist with web hosting, domain names, links to organizational site, crisis site and servers, computer and software set up and operations, phones, text services, phone bank or virtual call centers, radios.

Team Specialist—essentially a Human Resources job for the crisis communication team. Provides adequate trained team members, identifies upcoming needs including for transitions and extended events. Meets needs of team members including food, rest, bathroom facilities, etc.

Facilities, Equipment, Supplies—Provides these items as identified in the list.

Security—Security can be a major concern depending on the event. Security may be needed to control access to the team workspace, to locations where

Documentation & Administration -- If your organization does not require detailed records of the activities and decisions involved in a major crisis, it should. Government responses require detailed documentation for good reason. These records may be important for legal purposes but can be invaluable for the in-depth analysis of an event that is an essential part of good crisis management. The Support unit will establish and insure compliance with the reporting and documentation requirements of the organization and/or the Communication Lead. It may be advisable, particularly in the intense part of a response, to have documentation specialists assigned to the units to provide this documentation support for them.

There always seems to be a need for administrative assistance to help with a wide variety of tasks. Some of these tasks including liaison work, or serving as "runners," to deliver messages or documents to team members who may be physically separated. Sometimes these people are necessary to assist with producing materials such as copying materials for up coming public meetings or press conferences or picking up printed materials from an outside printer. Having a few qualified administrative assistants available will often pay major dividends.

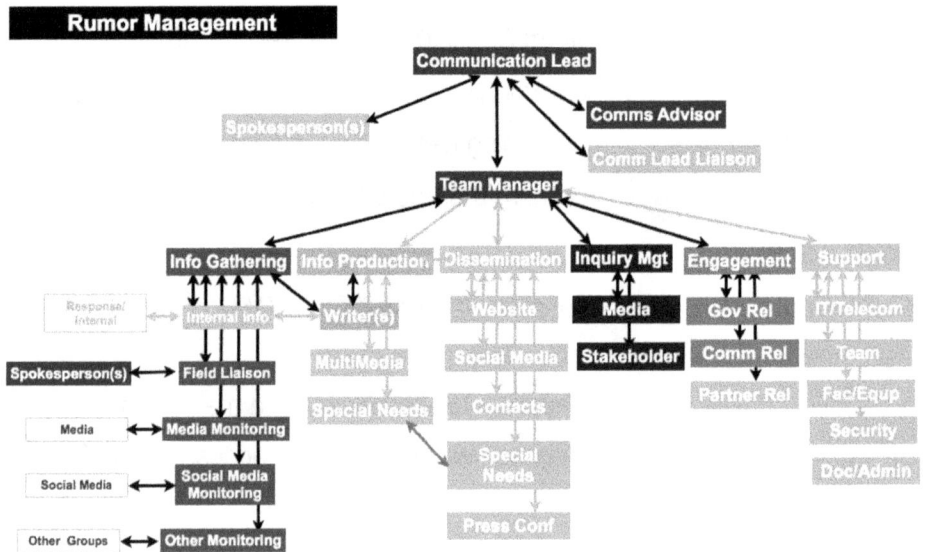

Rumor Management

The entire plan comes into focus in the increasingly important task of rumor management. Ten years ago I used to preach that the goal of crisis communication was to be the first and best source of the information about your event, borrowing from the US Coast Guard's excellent policy. But now it is clear in most events you simply can't be first. Unless the event is completely hidden from those with smartphones, text capability and cameras, the story will told by those first experiencing the event. But, as is often stated, what is said and reported about an event is usually wrong-- particularly in the early stages. That means that you and your crisis communication team who represent the organization at the heart of the crisis need to be the primary authority, the credible source of information and the deliverer of official messages. And that means that rumor management becomes job number one.

Rumor management begins with listening. As you can see from the graphic, listening is not just done by the Information Gathering team even though they are the central focus of it. Anyone who has the opportunity to engage with those outside have the obligation and opportunity to listen. That includes the Inquiry Management team and the Engagement team in particular. It also includes the Spokesperson and the Field Liaison.

It is the responsibility of the Info Gathering Lead to make certain rumors are identified, analyzed and brought to the attention of the Team Manager and the Communication Lead. However, to speed the process of creating appropriate responses, the rumors are also delivered to the Information Production Lead and/or Writers to enable a quick start on producing responses. It is up to the Communication Lead and Team Manager to determine how best to respond and also how far to delegate responsibility for fast responsive without requiring approvals. Clearly, significant rumors that have "legs" and can significantly misinform the public and stakeholders need fast and completely accurate responses and those responses need to be aggressively disseminated using all available channels.

Phase 6: Transitions and Deactivation

The final phase deals with managing transitions between team members in protracted events and moving from a crisis mode back into "normal" operations.

Transitions

Planning requires assuming that events will be protracted. Most events are of relatively short duration in their most intense phase when the attention of the media and the world are on them. It's during this phase that the full Red communication team would be activated. But, today with so much information available, the intense phase is both very intense and relatively short. Many crises fall into the category that Pew Research has designated "one week wonders." The event may continue for some time, as we will talk about under Deactivation, but the staffing needs are considerably less during the wind-down phase.

However, it is also true that a significant number of major events in the past few years have been exceptionally protracted. These include large environmental events, product recalls and safety concerns, large-scale natural disasters, social media-centered reputation crises and others. That's why it is essential that a sufficient large team of qualified communicators be identified. Your event scenarios can serve as a guide to identifying the potential protracted events.

Planning staffing needs

This plan suggests a maximum shift length of twelve hours and a maximum duty tour of two weeks without an extended break. Because many events are global in nature and work must continue around the clock sufficient staff must be available for two shifts per day, and an entirely new team for replacement every two weeks. A shift from 8 pm to 8 am can generally be staffed at a lower level if the attention is focused on North America, for example. Assuming only that staff levels can be at 50% during the "off hours" it still means that if your plan calls for a crisis communication team of 30, you will need at least 45 including transition times. And, if the event is protracted, the 45 team members needed jump to nearly 100.

Transition times

Managing team members and replacements means planning for transition times between shifts and tours of duty. It simply won't do to have a new team member show up, be assigned a role and have the person who was filling that role say "good night and good bye." There must be plenty of time allowed for a thorough debrief on what has occurred during the past shift, the status of current work, information about upcoming plans, events, schedules, etc. Two hour transition time is best however at least one hour minimum is required. Team members should be briefed by the Team Manager on the importance of managing this transition including making notes throughout the shift to share with the replacement team member.

Transitions between duty tours is even more critical as the team member being relieved will likely not be accessible for questions after they have left. A half day transition is minimum, allowing time for them to work together, share all relevant information, attend briefing meetings together. The relieving team member should be strongly encouraged to ask as many questions as possible and take notes.

Deactivation

Deactivation is complete when the organization has returned to business as usual or, as is often the case, a "new normal." Communications about the event become part of the routine communications function and not operated as a separate operation. Deactivation is not completed until After Action Reports and opportunities to learn from the event have been completed.

Deactivation takes much longer than most anticipate. The most important thing to realize about deactivation is that the event is not over just because the last satellite truck has pulled out of the parking lot or the last press conference has been completed. Too many believe that once the mainstream media have moved on to other topics the event is over. One organization shut down their crisis website after media attention had waned despite getting over 20,000 visits per day to the site. This organization would never have considered shutting down a phone number that was receiving 20,000 calls per day, but because media attention had lessened, they believe the communication task was done. The event will likely hold the interest of some of your most important stakeholders long after the roving eye of major media lands on something newer and more interesting.

The graphics below illustrate the changes in crises in the past few years, particularly with the very significant role that the Internet plays in these events.

Yesterday: slow start, fast end   Today: fast start, slow end

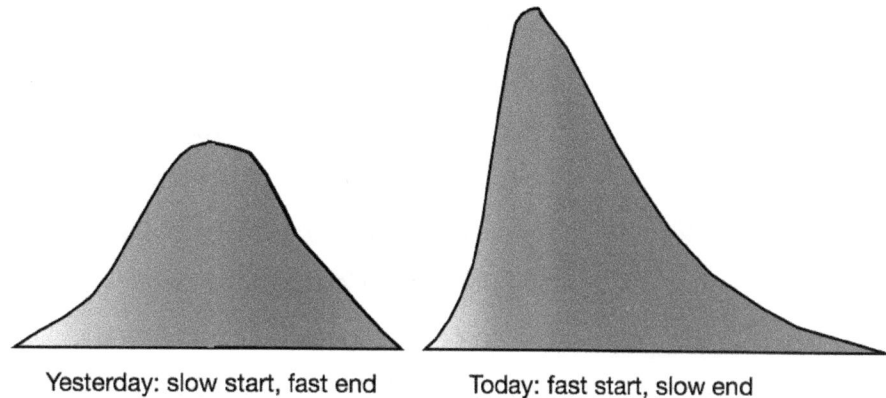

Yesterday's crisis

The first graphic shows a typical organizational crisis of the past. A relatively long initiation period, followed by a fairly lengthy intense period, and a short wind-down. This pattern was driven primarily by the news media and how they covered major stories.

Today's crises

In comparison, crises today are driven largely by the Internet and social media. There is a very short initiation period, sometimes literally minutes. The intense period with maximum media coverage and social media activity is more intense than before, but also tends to be shorter in duration. The key difference, however, is "the long tail." The wind-down period tends to be much longer because of the direct communication with those most affected and the continuing levels of social media interaction long after the major media have moved onto more current stories.

As activation was a process of placing team members where they were most needed in the organization structure, deactivation decreases team members as the needs in each of the units diminish. Because of the "ooh, shiny" nature of today's media coverage, the first unit that will likely see a reduced need is for the Media Inquiry section of the Inquiry Management unit. This also means that the need for updates on the frequent schedule that has been established will likely diminish. If the event itself has begun to wind down, the information about the response will decrease as will the need for the internal sections of the Information Gathering unit. Because of the likelihood of continuing stakeholder inquiries and interest and the need for on-going engagement with stakeholders, the Stakeholder Inquiry section and the Engagement unit may be decreased at a lower rate.

The Team Manager makes reassignments as the need for team members is reduced, reassigning key team members to different areas and releasing from service the team members that are not part of the core crisis communication team.

The Support Lead assumes responsibility for decommissioning the supplies, equipment and facilities when they are no longer needed.

Learning lessons

After Action Report and Lessons Learned

There are so many things to be learned during a major crisis. Yet, few organizations make the effort to capture the important lessons and share them to help prevent future crises and improve future responses. While creating a Lessons Learned document or After Action Report is very important, it is a wasted exercise if it does not include how it will be used to make needed changes. The organization leaders need to commit to reviewing the reports, modifying policies, plans, and procedures as warranted, review response team performance and make necessary changes, and communicate to the organization the key items learned and what has been done to improve.

The After Action Report should focus on a few key items, and knowing before the event what those items are will help response leaders and crisis communication team leaders during the event. Here are a few questions to be used in construction your After Action Report:

What was the overall goal of the communication effort? (Examples: to protect and build public and stakeholder trust, to protect brand value, to protect share price...)

Were we successful? How measured?

How well were the goals of the response articulated by the response leaders?

How well did the crisis communication effort meet those goals?

What was greatest contributing factor to our success?

What contributed most to our inability to achieve the goal(s)?

List all the major units. Grade performance on a scale of 1-10. Explain primary reasons for the grade.

List all unit leaders. Grade performance on a scale of 1-10. Explain primary reasons.

Identify any messages, channels or strategies that were particularly effective. Identify any that were strongly disappointing.

What worked well that must be retained?

What must be changed in order to improve response?

Final Thoughts

I started the introductory video that accompanies this manual near the spot where in 1999 a gasoline pipeline exploded and three young lives were lost. The ideas, strategies and tactics described in here are a result of the journey in crisis management that I've been on since that terrible day. But as I write these words and think back again on that event, I am reminded that almost every crisis or emergency is a human tragedy of some kind. Lives can be lost or forever altered. Lifetimes of hard work can be shattered in moments. Innocent people can be harmed. The environment and all things we value can be lost or severely damaged.

Crisis and emergency management is ultimately about people, relationships and protecting the most important things in our lives and the world around us. Doing our job well will not only help prevent terrible things from happening, but will help us protect lives, health, reputations, our communities and possessions.

With this manual and the thoughts contained in them, I wish for you the very best which is that nothing bad happens. But, if it does, I wish for you the strength, courage and clear thinking needed to protect yourself, your loved ones, the people around you and all that we hold dear.

Gerald Baron
Bow, Washington
2012

About the Author

Gerald Baron has become one of the most widely recognized voices in crisis and emergency communications through his writings and technology innovation. As the president of a marketing and public relations firm in Washington State he became involved in managing communications during a major pipeline explosion in 1999. That experience led him to develop the PIER System (Public Information Emergency Response) which is the most widely adopted crisis and emergency management technology. It also led him to write *Now Is Too Late: Survival in an Era of Instant News*, originally published in 2002 and updated in 2006. This has been called "the best guide to crisis communications in the digital era" by a leading communication expert. His blogs, "Crisis Comm" for Emergency Management, and "Crisisblogger" have earned a wide following in the crisis and emergency management communities.

Through PIER, Mr. Baron has worked with numerous communication leaders from federal, state and local government agencies and a number of the world's largest and most well-known companies. He has developed crisis and emergency communication plans for dozens of government agencies, particularly regional coordinated communication plans for large metropolitan agencies as part of the Urban Area Security Initiative. He has also developed global and regional communication plans for Fortune 100 companies, global non-profits and the nation's largest public utility.

Agincourt Strategies LLC was founded in 2011 to continue to the work of addressing the challenges of matching technology and strategy to the ever-changing world of crisis communication, issue management and stakeholder engagement. Mr. Baron works with a team of highly experienced crisis communication experts to conduct gap analyses, write crisis communication plans, consult on issue and crisis response, and train communicators.

More to the OnePage Crisis Communication Playbook

The OnePage Playbook is designed to be a complete and comprehensive guide crisis communication preparation and response.

The entire program includes:

OnePage Guide and Playbook Manual
130 page manual that explains in detail each of the steps listed in the OnePage Guide.

Video Training Series
A series of videos, each 10-15 minutes in length cover all topics included in the Manual. Ideal for training crisis communication team members, the videos detail the workflow, roles and interactions necessary for effective response.

Online Quiz
An online questionnaire is used after completing video to provide assurance that the video has been viewed and that content has been absorbed.

Train-the-Trainer Presentation
Complete PowerPoint or Keynote slide series covering all topics in the manual, designed to enable managers to train all levels of staff on the OnePage Guide and Playbook.

Check www.agincourt.us for latest status on availability of these items.

Other Agincourt Training Products:

Social Media in Emergency Management
Video Training
Featuring Chief Bill Boyd

A series of videos approximately 8 to 12 minutes each detailing all major social media channels. Chief Boyd, a fire chief and Incident Commander, explains their uses and benefits for emergency communications and response management.

Innovative training and education for crisis
communication and emergency management.

www.agincourt.us
360-303-9123
training@agincourt.us

Agincourt
Strategies

www.ingramcontent.com/pod-product-compliance
Lightning Source LLC
Chambersburg PA
CBHW081543220326
41598CB00036B/6542